To Love The Sky

by Mary Alice Beatty

Huntsville

ALBRIGHT & COMPANY

First Edition 1986
Copyright © 1984 by Mary Alice Beatty

Library of Congress
Catalog Card Number: 86-070480
ISBN 0-932919-02-2

Printed in the United States of America

Contents

I

II

III

EDITOR
Laurie Frost

LAYOUT
Harriette Murphy

Dear Reader,

More than sixty years ago I kept a running story of my life in aviation, a first hand account of Pioneer Flying, and I locked it in the bottom drawer of my wardrobe trunk in mother's attic where no one would find it.

All those years "My Book" has been in such good company with love letters and Hop Cards from Annapolis, West Point and Princeton, 1920, 1921, 1922.

What does one do with keepsakes? What should I do with "My Book"? Should I put it back in the trunk or should I throw it away?

I decided to do neither. I published it. Now, once again, "My Book" is in such good company, with a history buff and a book lover—YOU. Thank you! Thank you very much.

Mary Alice

THEN CAME A YOUNG

MAN IN HIS FLYING MACHINE

He taught me to love the sky and to feel right side up and upside down in the clouds. I learned to know side-slip, falling-leaf, fish-tail, ground-loop. And far up, where no one could see, we rolled, we looped, we spun.

The Jenny would rise from the field like a box-kite in an updraft and when we were high in the sky, sometimes as high as three thousand feet, he would cut the motor and in the sudden silence we would drop off and begin to spin towards the ground. As the spin tightened I could hear the creaking of the struts that held the wings apart, and I could hear the whistling whine of the wires that held the wings together. When the spin was even tighter the whistling whine changed pitch, higher by more than an octave, like a violin string being tuned to the point of breaking. The sky was filled with music.

When we ran out of sky he flattened out with a jerk and we bounced, dead stick, as Jenny bit the dust. Then he ground-looped in the high weeds till we ran out of momentum.

I told absolutely no one that Donald had taught me to fly, because flying was not for girls. Flying was for men.

It was the custom in Alabama that when a young man wanted a girl to marry him, he asked her, with gentle entreaty, "Will you be mine?" Donald never asked me that. He said, "Sweetheart, you are mine." And he staked his claim with a diamond ring. I never said I would be his.

When my mother saw my ring she gasped, "OH, Mary Alice! He is such a wild one!" My father stormed, "He will never settle down! He will be flying all over the earth and you will both be killed! I will not permit it!" All their plans for me were being blown asunder in the backwash of a prop.

But one evening, in a candlelit sanctuary filled with friends, I walked, on the arm of my father, down a long white aisle and my father led the way. I was encased in a bale of Chantilly lace so thick that I hardly could see through. There were groomsmen, bridesmaids, flower girls, ringbearers. And I said to the minister that for the rest of my life, forever, as long as I lived, I would love and obey Donald.

We should have lived happily ever after for we had everything, a precious baby girl, a lovely home, many friends, money in the bank. Donald ground away stoically at the real estate and insurance business. But this life was not for him. He became more and more restless and he talked of nothing but flying to South America.

He wanted to explore, by air, the vast regions of the Amazon basin and the Andes that were marked on the maps as UNKNOWN, those vast regions where no expedition had ever been (and returned). He wanted to fly over the Andes and over the jungles where no plane had ever flown (and returned). He vowed he'd have his own airline across the continent of South America. He was so certain, he was so positive that he would.

I said, "When you fly over the Andes and over the jungles, take me with you."

8

He said he sure as hell would. And I laughed, because it was a crazy thought. But he said, "Don't laugh, Sweetheart. It could happen."

With my blessings, Donald liquidated all we had and borrowed all he could borrow to finance his Latin American Expedition. His plane was on order and cash was in the bank to see his expedition through. All went well, exceeding well.

FOUR   THE ITEM-TRIBUNE, SUNDAY, JUNE 2, 1929

N. O. Plays *Big Part*

N. O. Leaders, Route And Scene (

Flight Commander Donald C. Beatty Opens Headquarters At Roosevelt. South American Commerce Extension Flight Will Also Take In Central America. This City And Numerous Other Municipalities And Industrial Organizations And Firms Backing Great Project

A GIANT multimotored amphibian will take off in October for a tour of Central and South America with the most ambitious trade extension program ever developed by American business interests as its mission. The South American Trade Extension Flight, as this air tour is called, has opened headquarters at the Hotel Roosevelt, with Lieutenant Donald C. Beatty flight director, in charge.

New Orleans merchants and manufacturers are keenly interested in the tour and the advisory board includes Crawford H. Ellis and Lester F. Alexander, both of

UNUSUAL PHOTOGRAPH OF RIO DE JANEIRO SHOWING OLD AQUEDUCT IN FOREGROUND AND SUGAR LOAF MOUNTAIN IN BACKGROUND. RIO DE JANEIRO WILL BE ONE OF IMPORTANT TRADE CENTERS VISITED BY THE SOUTH AMERICAN TRADE EXTENSION FLIGHT

June 2, 1929

Then came October 29, 1929. Out of our beautiful, clear blue sky came October 29th, 1929. Screaming headlines, STOCK MARKET CRASHES! WALL STREET IN SHAMBLES! WIPE OUT! FORECLOSURES, BANK FAILURES! PANIC! SUICIDES! The stock market crash of '29 had occurred. The GREAT DEPRESSION had begun.

So suddenly, Oh so suddenly, all we had was gone! Gone was our savings account. Gone was our checking account. Gone were the funds for the Latin American Expedition for our bank, the Bank of Ensley, had been one of thousands of banks to suddenly close its doors in failure. Gone, for us, was everything. Only remaining to us were bank notes that had to be paid in the near future.

Strange, Donald felt no panic. Shock did not take him over. He said calmly that we would sell our home, move to New York City and he would begin again. He would interest others, as he himself was interested, in air transportation in South America.

It was a long, hard two years, harder than anything we had ever known, New York City in the depth of the depression. It was a time I do not care to write about, nor to think about. But strangely, Donald, Madelyn, and I were not unhappy.

We found a place to live in Brooklyn Heights, at the Pierpont, a new hotel completed just before the Crash. Our room was small but large enough to add a baby bed and a rented desk with a typewriter. There was a dog in the hotel that Madelyn could play with, a young wire-haired terrior named Nippy, owned by a man, W. O. Brown. Nippy was not a one-man dog. Nippy loved everybody, especially Madelyn, who immediately renamed him "Man Brown's Dog." Each morning I would take Madelyn, with her stuffed cat and Man Brown's Dog, and we would walk to a small park on the waterfront where the pup could run

11

and bark and where Madelyn could jump and scream, because they could not do that in the hotel. Then there was a man who came to the park every morning with a pony, twenty-five cents a ride.

Madelyn adored the policeman and his horse that patrolled the block around the Pierpont. Each morning he would lift her up to sit with him in the saddle. Then, when he put her down, she would stretch up high, on tip-toe, as high as she could, to feed the horse a loaf of sugar that she had brought from the breakfast table. It terrified me to see her hold out an open tiny hand while the huge brown beast opened his blue-black thick lips and lapped the loaf of sugar into his great yellow teeth. Madelyn would squeal, as though she were frightened. But nothing ever frightened my baby. It only frightened me.

It was as Donald had said, there were prominent businessmen of Wall Street who believed as he did, that the time had come for the development of air transportation in South America. After more than a year of trying to obtain an interview with Mr. J. P. Morgan, Donald finally was able to see him and it was then that J. P. Morgan enthusiastically pledged his financial support to the Latin American Expedition.

With J. P. Morgan's endorsement, wide interest and support of the expedition resulted. The Smithsonian Institution assigned Dr. Matthew Stirling, Chief, Bureau of American Ethnology, to the expedition. Seven nationally known scientists were assigned to accompany the expedition. The State Department arranged with the twenty-one republics of America for entry and passage through their respective republics, and the International Postal Union granted the expedition franking privilege. The Pan American Union (Organization of American States) endorsed the expedition, and the prestigious Pan American Society enthusiastically sponsored the project. The Navy

NEW YORK HERALD TRIBUN

Sailing to Picture South American Wilds

Herald Tribune photo—Acme

Members of an expedition departing yesterday aboard the Santa Maria to record what goes on in the hinterland of Colombia, Ecuador and Peru. Kneeling, starting at left, are Daniel G. Farrel, E. F. Mrovka and Dr. Matthew W. Stirling. Standing are Lieutenant Earl Rossman, E. T. Braman, Major Leslie G. Barbrook and John Verrill

September 25, 1931

Department, Bureau of Navigation, gave "authority for participation" and assigned Lt. Earl Rossman, one chief photographer, and one radioman as a Navy Unit to accompany the expedition. The various national press services gave wide coverage to the expedition, calling it "the most ambitious trade extension program ever developed by American Business interests."

From the *New York Herald Tribune*, 25 Sept. 31: "Professor Matthew W. Stirling, explorer and ethnologist of The Smithsonian Institution, sailed yesterday with six other members of the Latin-American Expedition, for seven months of intensive study in Peru, Colombia, and Ecuador. He hopes to trace origin of the human race in Canar, Peru. The group sailed on the Grace liner, *Santa Maria*.—

"Earl Rossman, who will have charge of all photography, spent two years north of the Arctic Circle obtaining rare photographs. He was with Sir Hubert Wilkins.—

"John Verrill, Harvard botanist.—

"Wesley Gordan Barbrook, former British major, field manager.—

"Cecil H. Villiers, noted archaeologist.—

"Daniel G. Darrell, assistant camera man.—

"The dozen men in the party will penetrate territories never before visited by white men, if their plans succeed. From the teeming tropical jungles they expect to wrench secrets which science heretofore has never learned."

Once again funds were in the bank for the Latin American Expedition. Our plane was being readied. Our plane, to be christened *SIMON BOLIVAR*.

When I said I was flying to South America with Donald, my father exploded. My mother wept. My friends forsook me; in their opinion, I was displaying a disordered mind. It was a most difficult time for me, but I was going with Donald, anywhere. My parents came at once, to take my Madelyn home with them, for I could not take her with me.

It is hard to kiss a baby goodbye.

BEATTY- LATIN AMERICAN EXPEDITION

SIMON BOLIVAR

Simon was a good-a flying boat.

The first time I saw Simon Bolivar he was sitting on the grass at Roosevelt Field, New York City's airport, and he looked like nothing I had ever seen before. Simon, the single engine, pusher-type Ireland amphibian seemed more of an arrangement designed to back up rather than to go forward. He was chunky and short-coupled, an ideal formula for ground-looping.

The engine was not where I had expected it to be, up front, mounted in the nose of the plane with the prop in reaching distance from the ground where someone could reach it, twist it and start the engine. Instead, it was

mounted back aft and hung high in the air from the upper
wings. This Pratt and Whitney WASP engine had all its
horses behind the cart.

Simon was built for rough water, rougher than I
cared to think about. His lower wings were outriggered
with pontoons, to help keep him afloat in the waves. His
massive hull, with high prow for high seas, had a broad
black bellyband lettered LATIN AMERICAN EXPEDI-
TION, which gave Simon the dignity of stout purpose.

It was a boat! Not an aeroplane! Although it claimed
to be both, how could it be either? Would it get off the
ground? If it did, would it stay in the air? I did not believe

Tony was always thinking.

it would fly and I thought it would sink. But Tony said, "It is a good-a flying boat." And we were to learn that Tony was right.

And we were to learn that Simon had a mighty voice and that he thundered into a stump-filled field, or onto a wild sea, with the gliding angle of a ton of bricks. We were to learn that Simon had an insatiable appetite for gas and oil and that he ground-looped with every chance he got. And worse, Simon had no landing gear brakes. Extension and retraction of the landing gear was manually operated by means of a crank that sometimes jammed. Once, this almost cost us our lives. Simon had a bag of tricks all his own, tricks that none of us had ever seen before. But Tony was right. Simon was a good-a flying boat.

Tony Peria, aeronautical engineer, assigned to the Latin American Expedition, was recently from "The Old Country" and he carried his Italian language with him wherever he went. In his late twenties, he was heavyset with jet black curly hair and shining black eyes. He was a hard taskmaster, demanding perfection of workmen and everyone else. Should a mechanic blunder Tony would mutter, under his breath, "Block-a head!" He had but one love, flying boats.

Tony had spent six months preparing our plane for the expedition. Simon had been a luxury four-seater owned by Otto Kahn but Tony had stripped it of all its finery and comfort. He had removed the back seats and had installed extra gas tanks in their place. Then, since the seats would not fit back over the tanks, he dismissed the idea of sitting on seats as an extravagant and unnecessary indulgence and announced, with finality, that we would "sit-a on the gas tanks." And that is exactly what we did. We sat-a on the gas tanks all the way to South America.

Donald, Jack, and I walked around Simon, examining the many modifications Tony had made. Jack, co-pilot

Lieut. DONALD C. BEATTY, MR. JACK WHITNEY *and* MR. JOHN L. MERRILL, *president of All America Cables and of the Pan American Society.*

for the expedition, objected violently to the removal of comfort and finery for he was a Whitney who enjoyed the luxuries of life and resented giving them up. Jack, not yet twenty, held a pilot's license, which few pilots held. He was an excellent pilot and owned two planes. New York newspapers pronounced him "Social Blue Blood." He had that Princeton look and he had that bored look, which is not uncommon among very rich young men.

I wondered what interest he might have had in such an expedition. I asked him and he replied that his greatest interest in the expedition was to get it over with and get the hell back to New York. "Then why on earth are you going, if you don't want to go?"

"Aunt Margaret thought it would make a man out of me. It was Aunt Margaret's idea, not mine."

It was indeed Aunt Margaret's idea. She was a Morgan and she had persuaded J. P. that it would be a fine thing for a young man like Jack to go as co-pilot on such a venture. So Mr. Morgan had put Jack, along with his financial backing and influence, into the Latin American Expedition.

Jack had but two loves in his life, airplanes and platinum blond show girls, both of which he could afford without scrimping.

For a long time I walked around and looked at Simon Bolivar and wondered how we could get to South America and back, in this contraption, with Italian genius Tony, wealthy playboy Jack, and Donald, all three of them encapsulated in Simon, with no elbow room.

And then there was me—I aspired to bring back recorded music of Amazonia. The men had discussed the possibility of recording the music of the Jivaro, but this project had to be eliminated for sound equipment was huge and heavy and required electrical current to operate, which meant that a power supply unit would have to be

21

JUILLIARD
SCHOOL OF MUSIC

(AUGUSTUS D. JUILLIARD FOUNDATION)

JOHN ERSKINE, *President*

INSTITUTE OF MUSICAL ART
120 Claremont Avenue
New York City

—

Telephone: Monument 2-9336
Cable: Musartin

—

FRANK DAMROSCH, *Dean*

October 12th, 1931.

       This is to introduce Mrs. Mary A. Beatty who is accompanying her husband on a scientific expedition which is to study the ethnological points of interest in South America. Mrs. Beatty has been educated musically and intends to study the music and musical instruments of the Indians with whom the expedition comes in contact. I believe that she is well qualified to do this work and I can recommend her as an intelligent and able worker in this field.

Frank Damrosch
Dean,

taken along also. It would be impossible to carry all this, and so the music of Jivaro would have to remain still another UNKNOWN to be left behind in the jungles.

However, with my training in music dictation, I myself should be able to record the music of the jungles. So, armed with high hopes, innoculations, staff paper and pencils, and with credentials from Dr. Damrosch of Juilliard, I joined the Latin American Expedition.

22

TAKEOFF FOR
SOUTH AMERICA

And now, for all of us, TAKEOFF was here!

Our departure for South America actually began on Fifth Avenue, for the Pan American Society had made certain that the takeoff of the Latin American Expedition would be an auspicious occasion. When we arrived at the predetermined location, newsmen, a motorcycle police escort, and an entourage of black limousines filled with top-hatted dignitaries awaited us. We got into our designated limousines and the auspicious occasion began.

There was a final check to make sure everyone was in his prescribed place, according to protocol; then the entourage moved slowly ahead of us to form a procession. When all was in perfect order, the police motorcycle engines blazed into action and with sirens screaming, they cut a narrow lane through New York City's thick traffic to let us pass. They led the way, at high speed, swerving and weaving between the piers of the elevated trains and we followed in hot pursuit, our tires screeching as we skidded the corners. Pedestrians jumped back, cars jammed brakes, a cart-peddler scurried for cover with his load of fresh fruit, and a bearded man shook his fist at the top-hatted dignitaries who dashed with us to Roosevelt Field

23

to wish us Godspeed.

Our plane, with motor turning over, was on the line when we arrived, and in the formal christening by Mr. John L. Merrill, President of the Pan American Society, Mr. Merrill said, "The Pan American Society is dedicated to the cultivation of a sincere friendship and true understanding between the twenty-one republics of America, and we rejoice that this expedition has been undertaken and hope that it will play an important part in further cementing the delightful relations already existing between these countries and the United States." In his concluding words in christening this ship of science and adventure, Mr. Merrill said, "May this mighty plane be worthy of the name it bears. With deep affection for the name of the great Liberator, I christen thee *SIMON BOLIVAR.*"

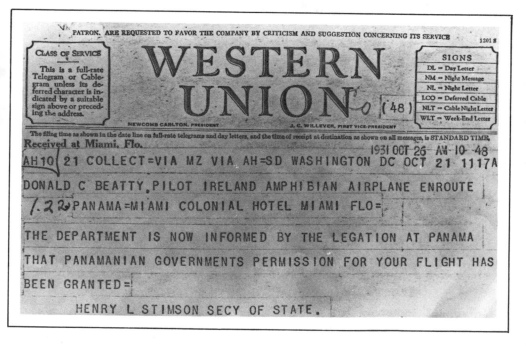

TELEPHONE WHitehall 4—5283

CHAPTERS

CHICAGO
WALTER W. HEAD, PRESIDENT

OFFICERS

HONORARY PRESIDENTS
HENRY L. STIMSON   JACOBO VARELA
JOHN BASSETT MOORE   SEVERO MALLET-PREVOST

LOS ANGELES
JOHN G. MOTT, PRESIDENT

PRESIDENT
JOHN L. MERRILL

SAN FRANCISCO
CLAY MILLER, PRESIDENT

HONORARY VICE-PRESIDENTS
ELIHU ROOT   L. S. ROWE

VICE-PRESIDENTS
FRANK L. POLK   JOHN BARRETT
HENRY W. TAFT   BENJAMIN B. THAYER
ERNEST H. WANDS

TREASURER
ROBERT H. PATCHIN

SECRETARY
WILLIAM P. FLOWER

COUNCIL

SOSTHENES BEHN
SPRUILLE BRADEN
FRANKLIN Q. BROWN
A. W. BUTTENHEIM
NEWCOMB CARLTON
JAMES S. CARSON
G. P. CHITTENDEN
ELIAS A. DE LIMA
D. A. DE MENOCAL
CHARLES V. DREW
GANO DUNN
WILLIAM E. DUNN
DONALD DURANT
A. STUART DURRANT
FRANOR J. EDER
F. ABBOT GOODHUE
ROBERT O. HAYWARD
R. W. HEBARD
PHILIP W. HENRY
THOMAS KEARNY
FRED LAVIS
JAMES C. LUITWEILER
SEVERO MALLET-PREVOST
S. Z. MITCHELL
JAMES M. MOTLEY
CHARLES M. MUCHNIC
FRANK C. MUNSON
GEORGE B. ROBERTS
JOSEPH H. SENIOR
WILLIAM E. SHEPHERD
D. A. C. SMITH
JAMES SPEYER
EUGENE P. THOMAS
ELISHA WALKER
THOMAS J. WATSON

THE PAN AMERICAN SOCIETY, INC.
(FOUNDED IN 1912)

67 BROAD STREET

NEW YORK

Address of John L. Merrill, President,
The Pan American Society, at Roosevelt Field,
Sunday, October 18th, 1931, on the occasion of
naming the amphibian plane in which Lieut.
Donald C. Beatty, leader of the Latin American
Expedition is to fly to Colombia, Ecuador and
Peru (for seven months of exploration).

We have assembled to bid Godspeed to
Lieut. Donald C. Beatty, who is heading a scientific
expedition to Colombia, Ecuador and Peru in search
of ancient ruins in those countries.

The Pan American Society is dedicated
solely to the cultivation of sincere friendship
and true understanding between the twenty-one
Republics of America, and we rejoice that this
expedition has been undertaken and hope that it will
play an important part in further cementing the
delightful relations already existing between those
countries and the United States.

As President of the Pan American Society
I have been asked to name the plane in which Lieut.
Beatty is to make this inspiring journey, and I rejoice
that the plane is privileged to bear the name of the
great Liberator.   It was he that blazed the way
in the long ago and made possible the establishment of
these Republics.

We bid a fervent Godspeed to Lieut. Beatty
and his distinguished associates, and we fervently hope
and pray for a most successful trip and a safe return.

May this mighty plane be worthy of the name
it bears.   With deep affection for the name of the
great Liberator, I christen thee, SIMON BOLIVAR.

TO DEVELOP GOOD UNDERSTANDING AND FRIENDLY INTERCOURSE AMONG THE PEOPLES
OF THE TWENTY-ONE AMERICAN REPUBLICS

Champagne splashed and we were off.

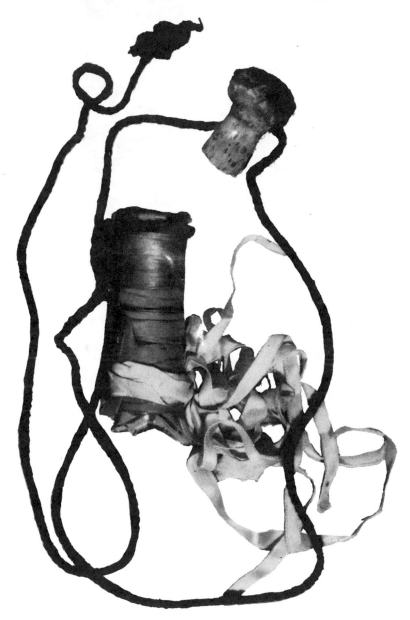

We were packed in the plane before the christening and, when the champagne splashed, Simon's motor opened up and roared like no motor I had ever heard before, as he lumbered down the runway and lifted off at the very last edge of the cement. However, once in the air, he gained altitude in normal fashion and I hoped that Tony knew what he was talking about when he said Simon was "a good-a flying boat." Nevertheless, I was nervous and uncomfortable as I "sat-a on my gas tank."

The gas tanks, though baffled internally, were not sound-insulated in any way. Every vibration of the engine was conducted and amplified through them, as though they were kettledrums. The never-ending thunder of Simon's motor paralyzed my hearing. I crammed my aching ears with cotton and I buckled my earmuffled helmet tight, to the last notch of tightness. But the thunder was not coming through my ears. It was coming through all of me.

My backbone reverberated with the vibrations that shattered my nerves. It was as though I sat on gargantuan electric massage equipment that had gone haywire. My whole bone structure seemed harmonic to Simon's roar.

Since the gas tanks were larger than the seats they replaced, there was not enough headroom for me to sit up straight. So I sat, hunched over. In a short time my knees and elbows cramped and ached, for there was no room to move them.

I sat, tightly strapped, straitjacketed to an unshielded, uncushioned, vibrating, shining, duralumin gas tank, as we winged our way to South America, for weeks and weeks. It seemed for years.

My father was right. I had lost my mind to go with Donald.

With every square inch filled with gas tanks, there was no room for baggage—each of us carried almost nothing. I carried only a comb, a toothbrush, and an extra flying suit, rolled in a bandanna and tied in a knot. The men carried an extra flying suit, a shaving kit, and small things of their choosing.

They chose strange things to take. Tony took a stiff straw hat with a plaid hatband. In our first forced landing, at Atlanta, he beat his hat to pieces in his alarm. Jack carried a most carefully rolled striped necktie in his breast pocket, but somehow it was lost in the commotion of our first night landing in Birmingham. I did not ask them why they took these things in the first place. In such close quarters we had to keep it pleasant.

The men wore loaded pistols at all times. (Jack's was pearl handled.) Tony's pistol bumped the gas tank and usually pointed straight at me, but I did not comment. Those loaded pistols were to get us in great big difficulties; in fact, they almost cost us our lives in revolution-torn Cuba.

There was no room for food or drink so we ate before take off and drank when day was done. It was imperative that we drink nothing at all until we landed for the night. Morning coffee was most definitely taboo.

All went well the first day. Once over the Mason-Dixon Line I amused myself watching the highways and small towns that I knew so well. Twice we circled very low and buzzed the home of a friend. Dogs barked at us, and chased us. I could not hear the barking over the thunder of Simon's engine, but I could see that they were barking their heads off. They were jumping in the air at us. A plane over their backyard was a novelty—and a menace.

Later in the afternoon we arrived in Charlotte, North Carolina. I was disappointed in the Charlotte airport for my grandfather had so much to say about it, he being from North Carolina. It was not an airport at all, it was just another flying field, but it was a good one. It was fenced all around to keep out cows and horses and it was well sodded. Donald circled only once and saw that it had no stumps, no outcroppings of rock, no ant hills. It was safe for landing.

We were met by the airport manager and gentlemen of the press who drove us into town in a truck and took us to the Mecklenburg Hotel. After dinner strangers came in to pay their respects and wish us luck along our way. And moonshiners came bringing gifts from their stills. It was no place for a lady, so I slipped off to bed and left the men to have a jolly good time with Mecklenburg Moonshine, White Lightning.

We were sorry that the airfield manager had insisted upon taking us to the field the next morning for we knew that he would be late. But we adjusted to the custom we knew so well and had our breakfast in bed.

It was a great breakfast: fruit, grits, eggs, ham, sausage, hot biscuits and syrup, pancakes and honey, milk and coffee. The waiter brought us our check for twenty-five cents each, which included room service. Later in the morning when we met Jack and Tony, they were flab-

The Charlotte Observer

CHARLOTTE, N. C., WEDNESDAY MORNING, OCTOBER 21, 1931   PRICE: FIVE CENT

Explorer Stops Here On Way To Wilds Of South America

Lieut. Donald C. Beatty Heads Expedition to Study Life of Natives of Upper Amazon and Napo Rivers.

Lieutenant Donald C. Beatty, formerly of the United States army, spent last night in Charlotte as a stopover on a trip that is to take him on a scientific expedition by airplane to the wildest regions of South America.

October 21, 1931

bergasted over the breakfast and the low cost of it. They mentioned it every morning for weeks and wished they were back in Charlotte for breakfast in bed.

We waited for the airfield manager until almost nine, and then we called a cab and drove to the airport. The hangars were locked. We banged on the doors but there was no one there to let us in. Simon was inside and there was nothing we could do but sit on the ground and wait.

About eleven the manager arrived, and Simon was rolled out to be gassed. But more delays. There were only seven gallons of gasoline in the airport tanks!

The airport manager couldn't understand the shortage until he remembered that, the day before, there had been an air circus in Charlotte. There was wing walking, and even parachute jumping. A pilot would take you up, "Five minutes, five dollars." The manager said, "If you'd been here you might of made twenty-five dollars a hop, what with all them seats." He asked, "Wouldn't you of thought five hundred gallons of gasoline would of lasted a week?" He put the question straight to Tony, who did not answer.

"The gasoline truck don't come until day after tomorrow," the airport manager observed casually. "Guess you all will have to lay up for a couple of days."

We couldn't lay up for a couple of days! Tony muttered, under his breath, "Block-a-head!"

The airport manager slowly pondered the situation. "I guess it would be all right if you drained the gas out of them four Jennys over there. The fellows who own them won't be flying no more until next week." We would pay him, the airport manager, and he would write it down and replace the gasoline when the truck came.

So with cans and buckets Tony drained the tanks of the four Jennys, but those tanks also were practically empty. He drained two gallons from one plane, eight gallons

30

from another, twelve from one, and only three gallons from the last Jenny in the hangar. He strained the gas carefully through chamois skin to be sure of no trash and water drops and, when he had finished, he stuck his finger in Simon's gooseneck tank opening, but he could feel no gasoline, for the tank was not that full. Then he stuck a stick in the tank, but only a few inches wet the dipstick.

What to do? Should we wait for two days or should we take a chance on making Atlanta? There were no landing fields between Charlotte and Atlanta, but there always always were cow pastures. However, Simon would find a cow pasture difficult for landing, due to his weight. Should the ground be soft, he would sit straight on his nose in the mud. It would be even more difficult to take off, and there again, where would we find gasoline in a cow pasture?

"Well, hell, we can't stay here! Let's go!"

It was afternoon when we took off. Donald climbed slowly, using precious gasoline to carry us forward, spending only a trifle more to carry us up to five thousand feet as insurance. At that height, at least we would have a choice of cow pastures, if Simon konked (ran out of gas).

However, the cow pasture was a godsend for the unlucky pilot who had to squat down, dead stick, for usually the pastures were large, without trees and with smooth grazing grass. Then also, the cows were dependable windsocks, for a cow always stands with the wind on her tail. It was said that she stands that way so that the wind would blow the insects out of her face while she chomped the grass. At any rate a pilot could depend on the direction of the wind by observing the tail of a cow.

But there were problems and disadvantages with landing in a cow pasture. One was that the pasture was full of large, round, squishy flat things (I prefer not to call the name). Should a pilot hit one, and he always did, it would

31

splatter the plane. Worse, if he had his head out the side of the plane to see where he was going, which was standard practice for forced landings, one of these large, round, squashy flat things might hit him in the face, which did occasionally happen. A plane could roll a long way down a smooth pasture and hit many of these things, even with fishtailing to stop rollout.

Another problem with landing in a cow pasture was the cows. They liked to lick the airplane dope off the wings and chew the fabric. Then the cows would get a high, a staggering drunk and would go dry, or even die. Farmers would sue, and courts would award damages. So the luckless pilot would not only have lost his plane, he would have also bought himself a herd of dry cows and maybe a bull that so suddenly had lost his usefulness—forever.

We watched for every sign, hoping for a tailwind to stretch our gas. We watched the smoke from smokestacks that blew straight into our bow. The shadows of the clouds moved towards us on the fields. Windmills turned their tails to us, heading towards the wind. And we watched clotheslines with sheets and long-legged underwear (flaps open) drying and dancing in the sun, waving directly at us, telling exactly what we did not want to know. We had a very strong headwind eating up our fuel.

Slowly the farms, with their cow pastures, became fewer and fewer. And they became smaller and smaller, as we approached Atlanta. One by one the farms disappeared entirely and small buildings took their place. Then larger buildings sprawled and skyscrapers came into view, as the heart of Atlanta spread directly beneath us. There were no more cow pastures. There was no place to land.

But in the distance we could see the airport. We could see the fenced-in, sod-covered landing strips. Criss-crossing the grass were marks made by tailskids and wheels of airplanes, taking off and landing. There seemed to be no cars or trucks upon the field, neither cows nor horses, nor dogs. Donald and Jack grinned at each other, for after all, we might make it, we were almost within gliding distance.

Joy! Over the landing field!

Donald circled cautiously to look for surface conditions, ground winds, or wind devils. Suddenly Simon stuttered, sneezed, coughed, and with a final convulsion konked. Jack grabbed the handle of the gasoline pressure pump and pumped violently trying to squeeze an extra cup of gas from the tank. But Simon held his tongue with a silence that proclaimed louder than words, "OUT OF GAS! COMPLETELY OUT OF EVERY DROP!" Simon's ear-splitting roar had ceased and the sky was full of awesome silence.

We were too low to circle for a landing approach, chimneys and rooftops were directly in our flight path. I watched a house rise up to hit us straight on, and I ducked under my flying suit, refusing to look, for I was in the middle of my second forced landing or my first crash. Would I walk away? Nothing but a vertical drop could put us on the landing field that was squarely beneath us, and I did not believe Donald would put a flying boat in a vertical. But he did.

I felt Simon turn on his side, two wings straight up, the other two straight down, and we dropped in a vertical fall, like a rock from the sky. One second stretched into an hour as I listened to the wind pull on the rigging wires in waves of crescendo and diminuendo, as a harp with a thousand strings. Overtones and harmonies echoed through the wail of steel.

I felt Simon jerk to flatten out, squash to the ground, and bounce into the air again; then his nose dropped and bumped the sod. I felt his wings see-saw, pontoons bouncing, his tail trying to reach earth. A wild wild fight with gravity! But Simon was winning. He threw up his nose and dug in his tailskid.

I opened my eyes and saw that a miracle had happened, for we had not crashed. But Simon was headed in a big way for the operations office, and he had no brakes. Tony was yelling, "HOLD HIM! HOLD HIM!" (That was when Tony beat his hat to pieces.)

Personnel cleared out of the operations office and ran to grab Simon's wing and throw him into a ground loop, for there was no other way to stop a flying boat that had no brakes. They spun us around and Simon continued to ground loop, around and around like a flying Jenny, missing the operations office by inches. Then he ran out his momentum and stood still, statue still. He froze in his cloud of dust. We too sat still, statue still. No one spoke for there was nothing to say.

The men climbed out and shook themselves a bit. Jack said, "Tony, what happened to your hat?" Tony shook his head sadly and said nothing. Donald looked around and said reverently, "Lady Luck, at your feet!" I climbed out and looked for some sign of reaction. The airport personnel had gone back into the operations office and nothing registered the slightest ripple in the day's routine. But if this was routine for others, it definitely was not routine for me. The dirt felt good under my feet, and I reached down and touched it with my hands.

It was too early to stop for the day but it was too late to take off for Florida. However, we had flown only eight hundred miles in two days and we could not survive such a snail's pace. If we stayed in Atlanta for the night, two hours of flying time would go down the drain. But where could we go in only two hours?

I said, "We could fly to Birmingham. It isn't exactly on our route, however it is only 150 miles and if we get there after dark it won't matter, for Donald knows every square foot of Roberts Field, every stump, every mole hole, and every outcropping of limestone.''

The men considered the idea and decided it was better than staying in Atlanta and it was a bit further south, so, yes, we would fly to Birmingham, even though we would get there after dark.

It was a beautiful late afternoon. We watched the lights come on along the way. The moon hung low and was full. When we reached the outskirts of Birmingham we could tell wind directions because the steel furnaces sent up smoke signals, and white-hot slag residue, dumped from the tipple, lit up the sky with a crimson tide and pointed up Ensley.

Then on to Birmingham! And Roberts Field!

As we approached Roberts Field our friends, who knew we were coming, had laid out a welcome mat. They had lined up their cars along the edge of the field, turning on the headlights in the direction of the wind. Buckets filled with sand and kerosene-soaked rags had been set ablaze on the outer rim of the field, for the field was small and beyond it lay trouble for any one who overshot. We landed in spooky shadows, playing it by heart. (It was in the darkness of this landing that Jack lost his tie.)

In this darkness my baby was there, for my mother and father had brought her. A few people had come because they never had seen a plane land by kerosene bucket flares. That night I slept in my own bed, where I had not slept since I was married. There was a crepe-de-Chine nightgown hanging in my closet and my Brownie box camera with extra film was on the shelf. I smuggled both my nightgown and Brownie aboard Simon. (They didn't weigh very much.) The only photographs from the trip (N.Y.C. to Panama, aboard Simon Bolivar) were made by my Brownie box camera. For, although the men carried fine cameras for the Expedition, all the film for these

Reception at Roberts Field, Birmingham, Alabama.

cameras melted in the heat and dampness along the way and was completely unusable for prints.

That night our friends had a big party for us, and Jack had his face slapped by a debutante for his inappropriate efforts. He was hurt and surprised, for such a rebuff never had come his way before.

Morning came and we took off in a buttermilk sky with a wind on our tail.

Alabama smoke stretched out like a tent over the mountains, for Alabama hid her wealth of iron, coal, limestone, and steel behind a smoke screen from her furnaces. We wriggled our way in the smoke through the valleys, between the mountains, as the compass and altimeter waved in wild alarm. Jack and Tony cringed, but I laughed because Donald knew every square foot of those mountains.

Simon shied along, like a young horse spooked.

The crispness of fall slowly melted into summer and the country, that only the day before was ablaze with magenta and polka-dotted with heaps of harvest, shaded again into green. Not the slightest intimation of approaching winter save the numerous coveys of birds that headed south in clouds of thousands. Miles and miles of countryside unwound beneath us, fenced and tilled and laden with highways.

Then Florida, emerald, filigreed with streams, the water medallioned with lily pads and so clear that we could see deep into the blueness of it. For an hour I had leaned against my window, marveling at what I saw beneath me.

I think the sunshine got into Donald's bones about the same time, for suddenly he nosed Simon down in a tight spiral to within a few feet of the palm trees and flattened out to skim along, inches off the water. Then, for no good reason at all, he took out after a pelican and chased him ashore. Thoroughly delighted with what he had done, he settled down to fly over the everglades, great tracts of wasteland, amusingly laid out in lots.

Even Simon got a bit temperamental in the sunshine and developed a complex for thrown oil. He spouted the grease at the rate of four gallons an hour and slung it all over himself and us, forcing us to come down in Miami to install a new oil pump, and forcing us to waste another two days of our precious flying time. Worse for me, the pump was installed where my feet had been, for there was no other spot to put it. So I sat with my knees almost

The world beneath us lay in fantastic indecision as to being land or sea.

under my chin.

We proceeded to Key West over the last dribble of land along the east coast. The world beneath us lay in fantastic indecision as to being land or sea, and it amused me to think of Florida as the last luscious drop of continent that had spilled and splattered into the water.

Donald banked Simon frequently so that we could see the ships that steamed or set sail under our sky path, and once he dived at a school of sea devils that flopped lazily just beneath the surface of the water. Then he gave Jack the controls, and we pushed through a bit of bad weather while Donald read "The Virgin of Babylon" in *Snappy Stories*, the pulp magazine that Jack had been so engrossed in all the way from Miami.

It was a glorious afternoon, and although I was safety-belted to the uncushioned gas tank—my backbone vibrating, my elbows and knees cramped and aching, for there was no room to stretch—my uncomfortable quarters could not mar the thrill of it all. But at sundown I was glad to sight Key West.

Perched dangerously on the southernmost tip of land sat so small Key West, protected by so big guns of the United States Navy. Donald circled over the Navy Station Harbor to announce our arrival and to claim our authorized right to land. He circled several times to spot designated landing areas, to observe wave action, to test for wind directions. Then he nosed down to the water, caught a wave and rode the crest, holding Simon's nose high from the trough.

Slowly Simon settled, lumplike, and windcocked into the not smooth water beside a cement ramp for beaching aircraft. His wheels were lowered and he snorted up the ramp and dripped dry in the afternoon sun.

The commanding officer, Captain Robert Tyrone Menner, was there to greet us and to invite us to stay at his quarters for the night. There would be a dinner party that evening in our honor, should we feel up to it. We thanked him but declined his kind invitation, pointing out that we had no formal attire, nothing to wear but the flying suits we had on. He understood our dilemma, a dilemma that would have become his embarrassment should we have showed up at his dinner party in dirty flying suits.

Jack and Tony were not invited to the Captain's quarters. They were escorted to the enlisted men's barracks for the night. They did not take well to this at all, but the Navy did not care who they were, for Jack was a co-pilot, Tony was a mechanic, and neither of them ranked. Mrs. Menner worried a bit when I told her that Jack was a Whitney. "Tyrone," she said, "perhaps you should have invited Mr. Whitney to stay with us. Did you know he is a Whitney?" The Captain thought a moment but did not comment.

"Aunt Margaret would approve of the barracks," I defended the Captain. Neither he nor Mrs. Menner knew what I meant.

"Captain," I changed the subject, "your tropical flower garden is breathtakingly beautiful."

"Thank you. I am told that it is the finest garden at Key West," he boasted.

"It shows the work of many gardeners."

"Yes, many. I am fortunate in having so many men to care for it. Pretty, isn't it?"

"Absolutely spectacular. The hibiscus are the largest I have ever seen, as large as dinner plates. How do you grow them to be so tremendous? What sort of fertilizer?"

"Army mules," he laughed. "Did you not see mules on the Army post as you came in?" I had not seen them but I knew they were there for I had smelled them. Nothing smells like a mule. I did not mention that, I only laughed.

It was a pleasant dinner, a quiet relaxing time. We retired early and I fell asleep almost immediately.

Somewhere in the midnight hours I was suddenly awakened by screaming and shouting and by the thundering of hundreds of hoofs. "Stampeding elephants!" I screamed as I jumped from my bed and ran out onto the upstairs porch that connected all the upstairs bedrooms of the commanding officer's quarters. The equally startled Mrs. Menner and I stood there together, in our crepe de Chine nightgowns, and watched army mules from the fort, as they thundered their way through the hibiscus of Captain Menner's priceless tropical flower garden. Everywhere cratered with mule hoofprints, every blossom smushed into the sandy mud, everything havoc. Screaming sailors chased the stampeding Army mules, calling them names I never had heard before. And the beautiful wife of the commanding officer had a few names of her own to call the army mules.

"Get those mules out of here!" she bellowed command.

"Yes, Sir!" came the respectful answer.

TAKEOFF FROM
KEY WEST

Before daybreak we were escorted by Navy officers to the ramp where Simon stood, readied for takeoff.

"Tony," Donald asked, "is the gas tank full?"

"The Navy mechanics said so," was Tony's response. But the question itself was upsetting to all of us, and Donald himself would make sure. He stepped up on Simon's wheel, then on the windowsill, to the cabin top, pulled himself, by bracing w res, onto the motor and even higher onto the wing. Then he unscrewed the gas cap and stuck his finger in the tank. It was full to the gooseneck, just as the Navy mechanics had said. However it is safest to feel that wet gasoline, even though the commanding officer stands by and scowls.

Reassured that the tanks were full, the four of us climbed aboard and I buckled myself tightly to my seat upon the gas tank. The motor roared for some time, then as we began to roll down the corduroy ramp I could feel, through the seat of my pants, the gasoline slushing in the tank. I found out later that, if I concentrated upon it, I could tell not only when the tank was full but also when it was almost empty. Also, I could tell many things about the motor, things that are not readily known by listening.

However I never mentioned this to the men, not even to Donald, for ladies were not supposed to fly at all, and certainly not by the seat of their pants.

Cautiously and gingerly we rolled down the too narrow ramp and into the too rough water. Simon was harnessed with controlling lines, and strong sailors held to them, trying to guide his descent into the surf. But what guiding lines and what men can hold against the sea? The wind caught Simon by the nose and flung him sideways. The next wave caught a wing and bashed it against the cement ramp. With great difficulty we were hauled back up the ramp for another try at launch.

The sun was coming up and I saw by the dawn's early light Old Glory going up the flagpole. So proudly it waved in a gale from the sea, as uniformed men stood at attention. The band began to play "The Star Spangled Banner," when all hell broke loose, as once again army mules, pursued by cursing sailors, stampeded through the commanding officer's flower garden.

A second attempt at launch, and a third. Finally we were down the ramp into the pitching surf, and the guiding lines were cast off. Donald gave Simon all the gas Simon could drink and the motor gave him all the power it had, but the sea gave him more than he could handle, for every time we rose to take the step a wave would lick up and drag us down.

We settled in the water for a time, as Donald's strength was spent. After a rest he shot the throttle wide and we roared across the water, lurching over the swells. Suddenly the nose dived under a wave, like a porpoise, deep in the water. Blue sea washed through the hatch and flooded the cabin. Donald cut the throttle and the nose slowly rose to the top of the water. He looked back at me and asked, "Sweetheart, you all right?" I said of course I was, but I think he didn't believe me.

By this time we were far off shore in the Caribbean and although the swells were tremendous, the breakers were few. Donald shot the throttle wide again, locked his arms around the wheel and pulled back with his total strength, holding Simon on the crest of a comber. Roaring at full throttle, we rose to the step and almost took the air, but the sea glued to the hull.

Try once more! We caught the crest of the next comber and, with a last angry plunge, Simon flung himself free and soared into the sky.

THE GUNS OF
MORRO CASTLE

It was my first flight out of sight of land and I shivered at the slightest sign of clouds. It was terrifying to see Key West disappearing behind us and to see only open tumbling ocean beneath. After watching for awhile I decided to turn my thoughts to other things, so I reflected upon the strength and durability of duralumin, and I observed the intricacy of a cowlick on the back of Jack's head.

After an eternity I sighted Cuba. LAND HO! Terra firma! Blessed Cuba! But how was I to know that we were better off and safer in the ocean? How were we to know that Cuba was in revolution and under martial law, and that no one flew over Morro Castle and lived to tell about it? Not knowing this, we flew over Morro Castle and we flew low.

The fort turned its anti-aircraft guns on us and I could see straight into the black muzzles that were holding us directly in their sights and following us in our every move. More anti-aircraft guns backed off then rose up and pointed long blue steel fingers in my face, and the muzzles of these guns followed us as the eyes of a snake follow a bird. I was held in fright and in charm by black eyes of gun muzzles. Dear God! Would these guns fire?

I watched two fighter planes take off and dart at us with unbelievable swiftness. They flew within an arm's length of our wing tip. Fierce-faced Cuban pilots motioned thumbs down and swooped around us. And as Donald cautiously slid away from them they closed in even tighter to force us into a spiral to the ground. What did they think this was, a Flying Circus? Did they not know that all three of us could go down in flames, locked together, wing to wing?

I looked back and a third fighter was directly on our tail, guns poised, in perfect position to blast us out of the sky. These were well trained combat pilots and their planes were the latest war weapons. Against them big, fat, completely unarmed Simon was as helpless as a wind-sock in a gale.

They drove us unmercifully, straight to the ground, and, on precisely the spot they demanded, Simon squashed to the grass at General Machado Field. Cuban fighters with guns still holding us in their sights circled tightly overhead, preventing in any way our takeoff.

Why were they putting on such a show? Why were we the brunt of the joke? Or indeed was this a joke? There was something deadly serious and bafflingly unfunny about it.

The instant we landed, Cuban gold-braided, gun-belted Army Officers surrounded us. They seized Simon, ordered us out, demanded to know, "Captain, by what authority are you in Cuba?"

Donald presented his entrance papers and he recited his words of felicitations to Cuba from the Pan American Society, a society of which they knew nothing.

But their belligerency became overshadowed with intense interest, their hot tempers became spiced with curiosity and amazement as they inspected Simon Bolivar.

General Machado Field, Havana, Cuba.

It was evident that in all their experience they never had seen anything like Simon. Cuban officers asked, almost politely, "Capitan Beearty, what sort of plane is theese? Como se llama?"

Cuban fighter pilots swishtailed to a sudden landing alongside, jumped from their fighter planes to claim their prize, their spoils of war. What was this thing they had captured? They saluted, they spoke most pleasantly to Donald, "Buenos dias, Capitan."

Cuban Army mechanics gathered around to help Tony look for damage that might have been sustained in the difficult takeoff at Key West. They shook their heads and said, "AH! Que lastima! Que lastima!" Tony shook his head and agreed with whatever it was they were saying, and I knew without being told that Simon was in a bad way. With such damage how had we remained in the air for so long a journey from Key West to Cuba! All who saw marveled at this, for ribs in both wings were broken and control cables hung loose between the struts. We were in Cuba for an indefinite stay, until repairs could be made, and, more unpredictable, until Cuban authorities would release us. Simon Bolivar, the Great Liberator, was himself a captive.

Donald, Jack, and Tony were visibly disturbed and shaken by all this, but first things first. We would get Simon fit for flying again, so we set to work, each of us doing, at Tony's direction, the job we were qualified to do. The men carefully ripped off the wing fabric and for two days they worked day and night to repair the broken struts and controlling cables. On the third day, Tony gave me a twelve-inch needle, a bucket of dope thinner, a ball of waxed linen cord, and told me to "Sew-a up the wings."

How could I sew up the wings! Never in my life had I! Furthermore, never in my life had I seen anyone sew up

Plenty trouble! Plenty trouble! Simon lay in pieces in a shed, injured by high seas at Key West.

a wing! Tony would teach me, but I being a woman should know how to sew without being taught. It was clear that he was thinking, "Block-a head!"

The sewing was not intricate; for although on a huge scale, it was about the same as sewing in a sleeve, maybe easier. (Sewing in a sleeve is not easy.) However, it was more like quilting on a frame, but the frame of an airplane wing, being so large, makes the sewing physically strenuous. Actually two people are needed, one to push the needle down, close beside the rib, another to lie on his back on the ground to push the needle back up, close against the rib. Being only one at this job, I pushed the needle down, then I lay down on my back in the dirt, where rocks and rusty nuts and bolts cut my shoulders, and I squeezed under the wing to push the needle back up. On and on, into the night.

Peanut vendor with billy goat wagon. (The boy and the author whistled thirty-two verses of "The Green Grass Grows All Around" as she lay in the gravel in the hot Cuban sun, sewing Simon's wing. Perhaps sniffing the airplane glue kept their spirits high.—ed.)

All this time I had to keep the fabric wet with banana oil so that it would stretch to cover the wing. The oil gave the linen the feel of being cut on the bias, like a Mae West skirt. But the smell of the airplane glue made me sick.

Also, sewing up a wing is rather like making a buttonhole, for while Tony instructed me in tying "clove hitch" knots with every stitch, close against the rib, a clove hitch is none other than a buttonhole stitch. Had he told me to buttonhole the wings, it would have saved much time and frustration for both of us.

At first I made a mess of it and I knew Tony would say, "Block-a head!" But I managed to straighten out the puckers with dope thinner, and I learned to seal the stitches and raw edges with a pinked linen binding tape. When I

finished I had the hang of it, as is the way with most things. One learns afterwards what one should have known in the beginning.

When I finished, even Tony said it was a good job as he scrutinized the stitches, one by one, and as he thumped the wing fabric that was drum tight and had a pleasant sound to his thumping. He was proud of himself for having taught me so well, and I wasn't afraid to fly with the sewed-up wings, even though I had sewed them up myself.

Sewing up the wings, although it took all day and far into the night, was not a boring job, for I enjoyed moving around more than I enjoyed being glued to a gas tank. Besides, this was something new to me, and I whistled while I worked. I whistled a silly song I loved, "The Green Grass Grows All Around." The song has thirty-two verses and a chorus.

I had company while I sewed, for a small black boy with a billy goat wagon full of peanuts took his headquarters at my side, and he sold me great big red-skinned peanuts, all shelled, ready to eat, and packed ten goobers to a paper cone. I learned to say *mani*, and when I said *mani* he shelled more peanuts and sold me another cone-full for a large Cuban penny, which he pocketed. He learned to whistle, "The Green Grass Grows All Around" and he learned to say, "Green Grass," and he giggled. Whistling and giggling is the same in Spanish as it is in English.

Few things are boring the first time around, while most things are boring the second time. However, eating peanuts never became boring, for each bite seems always to be the first, and repetition is impossible. What in life is so unboring as a small black boy with a billy goat wagon full of *mani*?

Night caught the four of us before we finished our jobs and we continued with the aid of power lights, for we wished to take off at the first opportunity. It was very very late, and we were very very tired when we went to the air-field bar to drink our reward for a hard day's work. My fingers were badly blistered from the heavy sewing and I was so tired that I just flopped down in an armchair and laid my feet over on their sides. We had a drink around and my feet got numb, then another drink and my teeth got numb. So I quit, and left the drinking to the men. Coca-Cola and rum—Cuba libra!

I had become bored with the company of men and I went in search of a woman, for maybe somewhere at General Machado Field there might be one. Women were seldom seen at flying fields, for aviation was a world for men, rough men, tough men, crude, just as the Lord had made them. There was no other woman at General Machado Field, I was the only one.

Then I saw Miss Livingston. I was delighted and surprised to see her again, although I knew her very slightly, only having been with her a short time in Miami. She was

Who is Miss Livingston?

in the same distress we were in, for she had landed in Cuba without entrance papers. Although she brought many documents with her, Cuban officials levied a fine for not having the correct ones and her plane was impounded. American dollars were on the way to secure release. She was furious about it, but quietly contained.

No one seemed to know much about Miss Livingston. She was very young to fly her own plane from New York to Puerto Rico, which she did frequently. She was said to be wealthy and to own large pineapple plantations in Puerto Rico. And she was the first girl to fly across the Caribbean.

"It is too much trouble to get into Cuba," she said. "First I have to dodge the huge swarms of buzzards, then I have to dodge the Bebe Jague ant hills that spring up over night. Now, with the red tape of entrance papers, I probably won't land in Cuba again."

She paid her fine and was on her way before the rain started. I never saw her again.

After a few round of drinks with the Cuban officials, we received our clearance papers and were ready to take off. Joy! Joy! But it began to rain. And it rained. For four days it rained. We could not go into Havana for our papers permitted us only to take off and not to leave the field on foot. There was no place to sleep. We slept in chairs, in Simon, and we got to the place where we almost slept on our feet, catnapping against a wall.

And it rained! Finally Donald said, "Warm him up, Tony." We knew that we were going to try in some way to get out of Cuba. We took off in the rain, a strong head wind, pea soup fog, and we flew skimming the trees until clouds settled on the ground. Then we climbed up a few hundred feet and kept going, Donald with his head out of the window trying to see. But he could not see, we were flying completely blind.

PISTOL PACKING REBEL GENERALISSIMO

Rumba!

Were we still over Cuba, or were we over the Caribbean? Who could be sure where we were, in such blinding rain and cloud coverage? Before we left General Machado Field, Donald had said, if the weather farther south was as stinko as it was in Havana, it might be wise to land on the south tip of Cuba and wait. There was an emergency field there, San Julian. To start out over the Caribbean, with ceiling Zero, not knowing what lay ahead, was to take a stupid risk.

Simon snored quietly in his blanket of murky mist, and neither Donald nor Jack seemed to feel apprehension about our flying so low and totally blind. After all, there was nothing in the air, not even buzzards in this sort of weather. The only plane we had seen in the air since we left New York was over General Machado Field.

The weather continued just as stinko as it had been. I pressed against my window, trying to see if we were over land or water, but I could not tell, for I could see no trees, no whitecaps. There was no marker as to land or sea.

Suddenly Donald banked and turned away in a steep vertical, as a ship's mast, with sails spread in the wind, slid close by my window. Over water we were! And low! He headed back towards Cuba, in search of the emergency field at San Julian. And, with his head out of the window so that he could see, he found it and we landed.

The world was full of woe. The men staked down Simon Bolivar and we sat around the small operations hut nursing our fury with Aquarius. Hours and hours, nothing to do but watch it rain.

Donald had found a length of rope in the hut, and he amused himself for awhile by tying knots and doing rope tricks. Then he conceived the idea of lassoing me for pastime. Jack immediately joined him, with another piece of rope he had found. It did not particularly annoy me, so I held still for lassoing.

The field manager, observing our boredom, decided he should do something about it. But what does one do in Cuba to fight boredom? Fiesta, of course! He was glad he had thought of this. After all, the arrival of a plane was a rarity. And now, with Cuba under martial law, who ever again would fly into San Julian? The arrival of American flyers warranted a celebration.

Tonight we would go to a native hut back at the sugar-cane plantation where we would make Fiesta. The women would cook dinner, an orchestra would come, and we would eat and drink rum. And we would dance.

"Senorita, do you like to dance?" he asked, hopefully.

"I love to dance!"

He rode off on mule back but he returned crestfallen, for while he had no difficulty in finding an orchestra, there was nothing to eat but cuchon, rice and rum. "Senorita, there seldom is anything to eat but cuchon and rum."

"Cuchon?"

"Si, cuchon,"—forty-day-old pig—well, maybe fifty-day-old pig, or maybe last year's pig. At any rate, it would be cooked in five different ways, so if we didn't like it one way, we might like it another. And there was dark black rum, first run from the sugarcane.

There were many guineas walking around in the open field beyond the operations hut, and the idea struck the field manager, "Maybe you would like guinea hen cooked in red wine, no? Captain Beatty could shoot one, if he cared to."

The men were all for it. So they drew their pistols and went joyfully out to shoot. They blazed away until all ammunition was exhausted, but the guineas squawked and fled, unharmed, into the canebrake. The shooting accomplished nothing by way of bringing in food, but it succeeded in attracting a detachment of the Rebel Army and the Rebel Generalissimo instantly showed up to investigate. He demanded to know, "WHO HAS A GUN?" He vented his fury in Spanish, such violent language I could not understand, but I knew that our troubles were many and serious, and I knew that we were under arrest, prisoners again, not of the Cuban Army, as we had been before in Havana, but of the Rebel Army. I was more than afraid.

The Generalissimo was a tremendous beast of a man with a black grizzly beard. He wore a bandolier of heavy bullets across his worn khaki shirt, and he wore a pistol on each hip, each holster made fast at the bottom with a rawhide thong around a thick thigh. He held his hands alert and too eager for the draw, and he was surrounded by his bodyguards with rifles pointed at us. His eyes were black and fierce and I never remember seeing a man who looked so savage.

I was not the only one frightened; the field manager was visibly shaken also, for he had witnessed the shooting, indeed he had, not thinking, suggested it.

"WHO HAS A GUN?" the Generalissimo demanded to know.

Donald apologized, "Generalissimo, we were only trying to shoot something to eat. We have not eaten all day. We are flyers, downed by bad weather."

"By what authority do you fly into San Julian?"

"Generalissimo, we did not intend to land in San Julian. We were forced down." Donald presented his entrance papers to Cuba and his clearance for departure. He recited felicitations from the Pan American Society and pointed to Simon. "Simon Bolivar," he mentioned the name.

The Generalissimo walked over to the plane. He beckoned to his bodyguards, who came at once to join the careful inspection of this thing they had never seen before. Interest was instant and intent and they, as had the officials at Morro Castle, gazed in wonder and amazement as Donald demonstrated the controls and described the function of the wheel assembly.

"Simon Bolivar!" The Generalissimo slapped a compatriot on the back. "LIBERTADOR!" "CARAMBA!"

He never had been in the air, neither had any of the bodyguards. Maybe El Capitan would take him flying, NO?

"Oh, but Si!" Capitan Beatty would be so pleased!

The Generalissimo was delighted with this prospect of flying and he accepted Donald's explanation of the shooting, along with an invitation to join our Fiesta at the hut on the edge of the canebrake. Joviality took over the huge warrior. He strode out into the field, drew his pistol, and with two shots, blew off the heads of two guinea hens for our dinner.

I was more than terrified, having him for a dinner companion. I was almost going to pieces at the thought, for I never remembered anything in my entire life that I was so afraid of as this savage looking man. I begged Donald to let me stay in Simon while he and the others went to the Fiesta without me. But Donald said, "Sweetheart, take it easy. Nothing is going to happen to us. We are American citizens and Uncle Sam protects us."

He added, "But whatever you do, don't offend the Generalissimo for we must get out of Cuba."

My father had been completely right. I had lost my mind to come.

But it was as Donald said, we had to get out of Cuba, so I put on my clean flying suit, although it still was damp, not having dried out from last washing. And I buttoned it snugly around my neck and wrists. I tucked my hair tightly under my helmet, and it was hot that way, but I wanted to put everything I owned between the Rebel Generalissimo and myself.

At about five o'clock we piled into a Model T Ford and bumped and bounced our way over a road that only a Model T could conquer. We stopped to fight an alligator that blocked the road, but finally arrived at the hut on the edge of the canebrake.

The hut was a square room with a dirt floor and was roofed with palm leaves that rustled as we walked inside. It smelled to high heaven, an odor something like that of a second class zoo with a slightly parched smell of skunk thrown in. A horse stood with his head inside the hut and a few chickens, dogs, and cats walked around inside, none of them "house-broke."

The rafters were stocked with sacks of rice, the mainstay of Cuban food supply. I expected a sack to fall at any minute, but miraculously they stayed put during the entire evening.

A small portion of the hut was partitioned off for sleeping and a long crude table filled the rest of the room. The eleven men—five of them black men—and I took our places around the table; I never had eaten with black men before and I, being the only woman, was honored by be-

Black rum, the first run from the sugarcane, flowed freely at Fiesta.

ing seated at the head. I was, in fact, being doubly honored for in San Julian women did not eat with the men, they ate in the outdoor kitchen. I theorized that the women had made this rule, for the men were so dirty, oh so dirty! Had I dared, I would have gone to the kitchen with the ladies.

The women brought on the dinner, rice, cuchon, and the guinea hens cooked in red wine. Nowhere had I tasted anything so wildly delectable. And I ate ravenously, not to please the Generalissimo but because it was so delicious.

Then a very large demijohn of rum was passed around the table and each in his turn took a swig. But when it reached me I simply could not bring myself to drink from that bottle that had made the rounds. I passed it on to the next man, hoping no one would notice. Evidently no one did, and probably no one cared, for laughter had begun to grow with the eating and with the drinking of dark rum.

After the dinner was over, the women folk came, dressed in gay attire. Powder, paint, and lipstick had been laid on with a heavy though unskilled hand. They crowded close to me and put their arms around me, admiring my wristwatch, my aviation wings, but most of all my wedding ring. They slipped their hands in mine in a most affectionate manner and we laughed and babbled, they in Spanish, I in English, paying no attention at all to the language barrier that was supposed to separate us.

Then the musicians came on horseback and the music started. It was a five black man orchestra; one played the guitar and the other four beat with sticks and with the palms of their hands on small homemade drums, on the table, on the chairs, on whatever they found handy to beat upon. Each thing one beats upon has a pitch, a sound all its own. This disorganized beating on things made a noisy background for the guitar—a noise strangely pleasing without harmony, but so monotonous! The music script for the entire evening consisted of two measures played over and over and over again until I thought I would go mad with the fiendish monotony of it.

The men sang to the rhythm and the women laughed, held their skirts and danced, but slightly. The men passed another bottle of dark rum, but drinking was not the thing tonight, for one could drink anytime. Tonight was for singing and dancing.

The men began to dance, then the women took up the beat. The floor sent up dust and the dogs and chickens fled the hut. Breathing came in rhythm with the beat and there was little smiling for this dance was a serious affair. "RUMBA! RUMBA!" they chanted in unison. I did not know what Rumba meant but it had something to do with the dance. And it had something to do with the eyes.

The dancing was as monotonous as the music, two staccato steps to the left, then two staccato steps to the right, then a wiggle. Again two staccato steps to the left, two staccato steps to the right, and a wiggle. Then came the crescendo, a tremendous wriggle, an all-out writhe. This could be repeated, ad libitum, as long as one cared to dance.

Rumba was all the things a Viennese Waltz is not, and I watched spellbound. Must one be skilled to Rumba? Must one practice at all to do it well? Who is virtuoso? Then again, who is not virtuoso? Still again, who has not done it in bed? Should I applaud this performance or should I hide behind a blush?

Then the blow! The Generalissimo would Rumba with me! He did not ask me if I cared to dance for he did not ask ladies what they cared to do. He stood before me, unsmiling, with his loaded pistols at his side and with the bandolier of heavy bullets across his open shirted black hairy chest. If this man touched me I would scream!

I stood up, realizing that not even Uncle Sam would protect me. It was for me to dance. So I braved it and looked squarely into his fierce black eyes. They were not so fierce. He was a young man, younger than I had thought. He was condescending to dance with me, accepting me in frank equality. My fears began to settle down.

The music heightened and the singing took on a gayer tone. Everyone seemed to be relaxing because the Generalissimo had decided to Rumba. They stepped back and gave him the floor. He moved at first cautiously, a bit uncertain, as though he ᵣ ₋d not to offend. What was so new to him as a piloᵢ' ₋ᵢe? And I also moved cautiously, for what was so new tᵒ me as a Rebel Generalissimo?

The music picked up speed and loudened and he smiled at me. He stomped the ground as does a young bull annoyed with restraint. And as I warily watched his eyes his fierceness fell away and I saw nothing in his eyes but wild and uncontrollable joviality. He was eager, so eager, for the dance.

And he danced! Jeepers, did he! He writhed to the floor, then he reached for the rafters and loaded pistols slapped his thighs as he stomped and stomped the rhythm with his feet. The orchestra played the same measures over and over and over and over and over again, monotony forcing the beat of Rumba into the air. And the beat was getting to the young Generalissimo.

He pinned me with his eyes (but he never touched me) as he continued to stomp, and I returned the stomping. He laughed his roaring laugh and I laughed too, for the Rumba rhythm was getting to me also. Had he ever danced with a lady? It was hard to dance like a lady with this rebel, and with the beat of Rumba in the air.

His black eyes, as did the guns of Morro Castle, held me in their sights and followed me in my every move. They seized me and I was held captive by black muzzles. Though try as I did, I could not escape them. He was smiling, arrogant, enjoying my capture, my uneasiness, and he was totally uninhibited by my husband's presence.

This was not a dance! This was a game, the age-old game that knows no language barrier. Dare I play? I dared. And I yanked off my helmet, slung it to Donald, shook loose my hair, and danced the Rumba, although I never had before. I met his eyes straight on, I followed his every move.

The singing heightened and he stomped closer to me. As I cautiously edged away from him he closed in even more until the bandolier of heavy bullets across his black hairy chest rubbed my flying suit. The chant, RUMBA! RUMBA! grew louder and louder as the beat came faster and faster, forcing us to exhaustion. But I held the beat and followed every wild contortion of the dance.

The Generalissimo bellowed with delight, but Donald was furious, absolutely furious. He yelled to me, most angrily, CUT THAT OUT!

The music stopped, the fun was over, the party ended, and we went back to the field in the pouring rain. Donald was in a rage, but I had done exactly as he had directed, I had not offended the Generalissimo. And I smiled to myself remembering how much I had not offended.

I was to be alone that night, to sleep in the women's quarters while Donald was to sleep in the quarters for the men, that being the custom. I was not too unhappy about this, for who wants to sleep with a husband who is furious?

The only bed at the field was to be mine. But I had seen this bed, a bare one with no sheets, dirty and indescribable, and I begged Donald to let me sleep in Simon. But they would have none of it, they would put me up in style. So I retired to my bedroom and Donald went with the men.

In the room with me was a grunting pig, a scratching dog, and a mewing kitten. A whinnying horse stood just outside my half-door, and strange noises came from the canebrake. A large black woman walked in and out of the room constantly, and I was afraid of her. As she came into my room for the thousandth time I said to her, "Yassum!

Senora!'' She said back to me, "Yassum.'' We both knew that something was wrong with our communication system.

I lay on the bed in my half-wet flying suit. I kept on my helmet and my shoes, trying in every way not to touch the mattress. Sleep was impossible and I prayed for the night to end.

Suddenly I realized that the large black woman had given me her bed, while she stayed up all night. This very kind black woman! I said to her, "Gracias, Senora.''

She answered, quietly, "Yassum.''

And I went to sleep.

Morning drizzled in. Rain, rain, rain! We were so miserably dirty, for there was no place to bathe. Worse, everything we owned was wet and there was no way to dry. Dirty-wet! How long, San Julian, how long!

They brought me a mule to ride during a brief let-up of the rain, but the mule was Spanish and knew no English such as "whoa.'' He ran away with me and the men had to chase after him and stop him with strong vocabulary. Then I tried to play with a kitten. He too was Spanish and knew no English such as "kitty.'' He was a wild little creature, not accustomed to petting, and he scratched me.

The Generalissimo never came for his ride, and we never saw him again. I hoped he had not been captured and shot.

Perhaps it was not raining in Yucatan or Honduras. We would go and see, for we had to get through. But how were we to know that this rain was the forerunner of the hurricane that lay in wait. Not knowing this, we took off in rain, optimistically confident of better weather to come.

At last Simon was in the air, sailing the Spanish Main, and I was leaving behind San Julian, forever. But I was taking with me something I never would lose, for my memory had snapped pictures that would not fade.

HURRICANE

Wednesday, 4 November 1931
What a Day!

As the tip end of Cuba melted into the horizon, walls of clouds gathered in all directions and closed in on us. Simon became unruly and wild in the turbulence, and Jack had his hands full with the controls, for he was not so strong a man as Donald, and Simon was for a strong man to hold. So Donald took the controls and we nosed through the last bit of sunlight that tunneled the darkness.

Blankets of rain came down from everywhere and washed up the windows as well as down and I caught glimpses of the sea writhing and foaming in violent convulsion. The wind slung us unmercifully, queer green-gold brilliance shone in the clouds, and the storm, waiting until we were at the point of no return, swallowed us up. The teeth of the trap closed.

I do not know how to describe my feelings. First came fright, deeper fear than I had ever known before, but it was beyond fear that I felt. For a fleeting instant, within this total violence, I felt the supreme Calm of Might. And I myself, unshielded, uninsulated, suspended within it, was a part of the Calm. The Supreme Calm of Might. Almighty God. How dare we call Thy Name, even in prayer.

For two hours we fought this hurricane, going only where it cared to carry us, but we were staying aloft and Simon did not split to pieces. Finally the hurricane tired of us and slung us aside into the sunshine where the Island of Cozumel, off the coast of Yucatan, was dead ahead.

The little island lay like an ivory carving on a pedestal of jade, with palm trees waving from the slim slightness of their stems. The sea was calm, for the hurricane had disturbed it not at all, and we landed in a lagoon of thick, still, black water. When I heard that a monster sea serpent lived there and came up by night to devour humans, I believed it.

The beach was strewn with pink-lined cockleshells and long arms of white coral that had been broken loose in the tempest and washed ashore. Brilliant, gleaming, light-green lizards darted behind shells and tufts of grass and cocked their heads at me in curiosity and apprehension, and I at them.

I could have spent days on this storybook island. But we hand pumped and filled our gas tanks from fifty-five gallon gasoline drums that lay on the sand and made a dash for Honduras, with the storm close on our tail.

As we flew over the southernmost tip of Cozumel, I saw marble-like archways and statues, hugged in by a fanciful fence, all glistening white, with the sun full on it. I grabbed my camera but before I could open it we were too far away for a picture. I think it must have been a cemetery with grave markers of white coral. I should have taken the time to look instead of trying to open a camera. Cameras are stupid things to pack. Memory is for catching pictures.

The northern cost of Yucatan was as white as Cozumel, and the water, so jade against the white coral shoreline, became splotched with sponge and dark coral reefs. Then came the swamplands, with their purple-black

67

Fifty-five gallon gasoline drums lay on the sands of Cozumel.

water in scrolls and curliques through the mud. And finally, the dense flat forest, too thick to penetrate with a machete. Everything green! The water bright green, the jungle dark menacing green, even the sun seemed to flood the earth with a jade flare. A veritable Land of Oz.

Then, as though stripped with a knife, the water lay gray, blue, black, and the coast of British Honduras scalloped before us. We flew, skimming the water. At day's end, Belize. Maps showed that it was more than a village for it had a gas dock and a real hotel! How long had it been since I had seen a bathtub! How long had it been since I had a bath!

But horrors! What devastation! Never had I seen destruction like this! Belize had been turned upside down and inside out, and lay in splinters, strewn beside the sea, for the hurricane that we knew only too well had come and had done its worst.

Shattered houses tossed in the waves, battered and broken boats lay scattered high on the land, and huge mahogany trees, fallen, crushed the remains. But our tanks were almost empty and, hoping to find gasoline, we landed in the water and taxied up to what had been a gasoline dock.

All people and animals were in deep shock and in trance-like numbness. Bodies of the dead lay sprawled on the beach and buried beneath wreckage, and the smell of death was in the air.

The gas dock was torn apart, oil spillage stained the beach, and gas drums, half-submerged, rolled in the swells and oozed gasoline that floated around them. One spark could have lit a blowtorch of further destruction. Donald cut the motor and Jack and Tony worked frantically to push us away from the explosive area.

We had no choice, for we could not hope for gasoline in Belize, we could only hope for a safe landing elsewhere. Night was rising in the east, and our only chance was to push on down the coast and try to reach an emergency anchorage that was marked on our maps. So we took off and raced with the sun to reach it before dark.

When we arrived there, the hurricane also had wiped away this anchorage, and there was only open sea and coral reef.

There was a choice: Would Donald choose to land now, on the ocean, and save what gas he had until daylight, when he could see? Would he spend our precious gas now, searching in the dark for a sandy beach that might or might not be? Which life gamble would he take?

It was Pilot's Choice.

I felt Simon nose down toward the dark water, and I knew that we would try to stay afloat through the night.

Simon pitched and tossed and his wing struts creaked and crackled, as the pontoons alternately struck the waves. Jack, holding to bracing cables and to the rocker arm covering, climbed high on the wing to counterbalance rolling. Tony, holding with his knees, threw out a sea anchor, and Donald was on the bow, putting out a second sea anchor. I climbed out of the cabin, so that should Simon sink I would not be trapped inside. And I held tightly to bracing wires that cut my hands.

Salt water washed over us and the roaring sound of sea was everywhere. The sun had set and it was dark. Simon, with motor cut, was sailing at top speed in the wind, dragging his sea anchors behind him. But we saw that he could hold his own in these waters of the Caribbean. With luck, we would remain afloat.

Donald called to each of us, to be sure we were there. All of us were. No one had washed overboard. The night would end and we had gas enough to search for a sandy beach at daylight. We laughed and we wisecracked, for was it not hysterically funny to be still alive?

With an overwhelming suddenness the sea lit up with a flood of blinding brilliance and I shielded my eyes against it. I froze in new shock. What had happened? Where was I? Was this Heaven? The Pearly Gates? Was I dead?

I looked into the sky where this miracle originated and I saw that the silver flood narrowed into the lens of a giant searchlight. I wasn't dead, but was I hallucinating? Or was that really a man-of-war? I wasn't hallucinating, for, yes, truly a man-of-war lay off shore and was offering us help.

RESCUE AT SEA

The battleship blinked us a message with its signal light and Donald responded with the dim flicker of a navigation light on Simon's wing tip. The man-of-war was a British battle cruiser and the captain had launched a lifeboat to assist us. We cheered, and we waited for the sailors to come. I sat on the wing as the waves washed over me, and Simon pitched in the narrow streak of floodlight that focused upon him in the darkness.

The lifeboat towed Simon, with us aboard, toward the shore to a small village that we had not seen in the darkness. The beach was aswarm with screaming black people, doubly excited over the advent of a plane, which they had never seen before, and with the advent of the searchlight that set off Simon Bolivar as a spotlight sets off a circus performer. We could tell by the boisterous noise, even at so far a distance offshore, that the mob was rapidly growing in size and that the wild enthusiasm of the black people had reached a high pitch. As we neared the beach, the screaming became frantic and frightening.

The lifeboat skidded up on the sand, and sailors, holding tightly to the towline in Simon's nose ring, jumped from the lifeboat and pulled us into the shallow water, where we pitched in the foaming surf. Simon's wheels were lowered, and the next wave lifted him and set him on the beach. Then the sailors, with great strength, and assisted by black men, pulled him further up on the sand, out of the reach of oncoming waves.

Preparations were made for staking down Simon for the night, high on the beach, secure from the rising tide. But the natives, in an ever growing state of frenzy, were determined to kill this thing that they never saw before. Black men, with weapons of their own making, descended upon Simon and had badly damaged a wing before they could be controlled. Most fortunately for us, the British Navy, knowing how to handle such a situation, quickly had it in hand.

I climbed out of the plane and stood on the flood-lit beach, alone and far away from the dangerous mob. I was cold in my wet flying suit, but there was nothing I could do about it; so I stood and shivered and tried to settle my frazzled nerves.

Black men and black boys thought of nothing but Simon, this demon from the deep. But little black girls gathered around me. They formed a ring around me and they stood, half afraid of what they saw. For a long time I watched them. Had they ever seen a white woman? Indeed how could they ever have, living as they did in this tiny isolated spot in black man's land? They showed no signs of hostility, for they themselves seemed gentle little ones who had known nothing but kindness. And as we stood on the flood-lit beach together, I watched the magic of wonder catch them in its spell. Simon held no attraction for them, they could relate only to me, who was just as they were, yet so terrifyingly different.

I thought, if they never had seen a white woman, maybe they would like to see more of me. So I moved cautiously to take off my wet flying helmet, and I shook loose my hair. A gasp went up and the ring drew tightly around me. I had done a foolish thing to show my long blond hair. I was frightened, I was cold, and I did not want to be where I was.

A British seaman, trained to be alert to such things, came quickly and escorted me back into the quieting mob of black men. Then, as Donald again read a message that the man-of-war was blinking him, he answered with Simon's navigation lights, accepting, with great pleasure the Captain's kind invitation to spend the night aboard His Majesty's Ship, the *Scarborough*.

HIS MAJESTY'S SHIP
SCARBOROUGH

A Woman Was "Bad Luck"!

Though tremendously grateful for the invitation to spend the night aboard His Majesty's Ship *Scarborough,* I lamented long and loud the fact that there was no way on earth for me to get out of my dirty wet flying suit and into a clean dry one before going aboard. Yet I was happy, no matter in what condition ı was, to be transported by lifeboat out to H.M.S. *Scarborough.*

We were a queer-looking foursome as we climbed the ship's ladder. So dirty, so wet, and so exhausted, we made an exotic contrast to the immaculate British officers in their white, starched, gold-braided uniforms. As for me, dirty, wet, worst of all—a woman! They were not expecting a woman, and half-clad seamen scurried at the sight of me, for was it not BAD LUCK to have a woman on board a battleship?

A stiff and stiffly starched officer showed Donald and me to the Sick Bay, which was to be our quarters for the night. They brought me dry clothes—a rough-dried sack-like gown—and they brought hot rum to warm me and to soothe my frazzled nerves.

The Sick Bay was a very small closet-like compartment. An operating table occupied the bulk of the compartment and was in the center of the room. There were bleached white sheets on the operating table and hot water and snow-white bleached dry towels in the Sick Bay. I chose to bathe and wash my hair before stretching out on the operating table to close my eyes and collapse in divine cleanness—with the dreamy smell of disinfectant in the air.

Captain Agar, knowing our exhaustion, sent word that after we rested for awhile he would like for us to join him at dinner in his quarters. Donald said he was glad to hear about food. He was hungry. None of us had had anything to eat for more than a day. I said I was glad to hear about "rest for awhile." Joy! Joy! Heavenly rest! Gratefully and instantly I sank into deep sleep.

After ten that evening I was awakened for dinner. I begged Donald to let me stay in the Sick Bay and sleep on the "cutting board," but he reminded me that I could not decline the invitation for I must not offend the Captain. So I reluctantly wrenched myself from my dreamless rest and we were escorted to the Captain's Quarters.

I wouldn't be so trite as to say that the Captain was young, tall, handsome, and much too attractive to be isolated on His Majesty's Ship in the middle of the Caribbean Sea off the coast of Honduras. He greeted us with charm and with great formality. He joked pleasantly about our "Ducking." He thought Captain Beatty had done jolly well to have stayed afloat in such a bloody sea. And he observed that Simon indeed was a blue-water craft. However, he himself knew nothing of flying boats. He never had been in the air, although he had a cousin who was in the Royal Air Force Command. Flying was a bit new, you know.

The Captain's eyes were a cool gray blue. I saw in them worldliness, and probably a bit of merriment. But mostly I saw in them perfection, perfection of propriety,

Commander A.W.S. Agar and officers on H.M.S. Scarborough. *Much too attractive to be isolated on His Majesty's Ship in the middle of the Caribbean Sea.*

of training, of self-discipline, and self control. He doubtlessly came from a long line of perfectly mannered Men of the Sea, for indeed how else, except through lineal descent, could he have attained such heights as Captain in His Majesty's Navy? For was it not true that the British Navy was the most powerful war machine on earth? And was it not true that the sun never set on British soil? The Captain's illustrious background was showing in his cool gray eyes.

The Captain's quarters were spacious and immac-

ulate—austerely elegant. The Captain's table was a
handsome highly polished mahogany one, galleried
with an equally highly polished copper rail. I was seated
on the Captain's right, and four handsomely uniformed
officers took their officially assigned places around the
table.

Jack and Tony had not been included in this Captain's
dinner for careful consideration had been given to social
position. I was startled that Jack Whitney, of all people,
had not been considered socially eligible. Had a Whitney
ever known such slight? Even a dashing Captain in His
Majesty's Navy could make a social blunder. No, not

really a blunder, for co-pilot is not equivalent to pilot; there is a great distance between them. And mechanic is still a greater distance away. These three levels among the four of us often made for awkward and embarrassing situations. Actually, there were four levels between the four of us; I being a woman had a level of my own. I never decided if my level was top or bottom. But it was most definitely there to be reckoned with.

Dinner was served formally from silver covered dishes, engraved HMS *Scarborough*. The cutlery was engraved "HMS *Scarborough*," as was the silver service from which tea was poured. Wines were served in silver wineglasses, but I did not know the names of any of the wines, for I had known nothing but prohibition in Alabama.

After dessert and coffee, brandy was served in large snifters, like the ones my grandmother used before pro-hibition. But in this most glamorous setting I was ill at ease in my no fitting, too long, not long enough, sack-like, rough-dried garb they brought me to wear when they fished us out of the sea. I felt like something that got caught and hung up in His Majesty's anchor.

And I was uncomfortable in this wide world for men only, where a woman was considered Bad Luck. I re-sented being considered Bad Luck, but I dared not show my displeasure; for whatever I did, I must not offend the Captain, else I be thrown off this dreamy battleship that smelled of gunpowder and disinfectant.

I sat silently, listening to the conversation of warriors; and I wished I had remained asleep on the operating table. I sat and warmed my brandy glass with my hands, sniffed the brandy that was too good to drink, and became resigned to being bad luck.

Brandy! Rum! Brandy! Rum! It was unreal that San Julian was so far away in only yesterday. Brandy! Rum!

Warriors!Warriors! Warriors come in all sizes, some for land, some for sea. Some rough—very rough; some smooth—very smooth; some cold—very cold; some hot—very hot. Young British Captains in His Majesty's Navy, young Generalissir ˏ in the Rebel Army of Cuba.

My memory br‸ ˏt me pictures, fresh with the rhythm still upon them. And the Beat of Rumba pounded in my heart.

It was getting late, morning soon would come when we must be on our way. Hearing the ship's bell confirm the lateness, Captain Agar called an officer to escort us again to our quarters for the night, the Sick Bay.

Through a squeeze-way from the Sick Bay were two bunk beds against the bulkhead and I said, getting into the lower bunk, "What a day this has been! Glory! Glory! Bed at last!" I observed, "But this is the narrowest bed I have ever seen. Are all Englishmen this skinny?" Donald said he did not remember ever seeing a fat Englishman, but "Sweetheart, move over."

"Move over to where!"

He squeezed in and I said, "Honey, the upper bunk is yours." But he didn't want the upper bunk and he wouldn't have it. He sure as hell didn't like bunk beds. Then I reminded him that these were His Majesty's bunks and that he should show them some respect.

If he were Captain he'd have better arrangements. I thought the Captain did have. However, I did not permit myself to speculate upon these arrangements. I said, "I did not believe Captain Agar when he said I am the only woman ever to spend the night aboard the *Scarborough*."

"Do you always know when a man is lying?"

I said yes, and he said then he never would lie to me. Would I ever lie to him? I said no.

"Then tell me the truth, you fell for the Generalissimo,

didn't you?''

"You mean the pistol packing Generalissimo?''

"That one. You fell for him, didn't you?''

"The Generalissimo wearing the bandolier of bullets across his hairy chest?''

"That one. You fell for him, didn't you?''

"The fierce fellow who blew the heads off guinea hens?''

"I mean the SOB who danced like a lunatic with my wife!''

"Ah, honey, you're getting mad again. Let's not fight tonight. A battleship is no place to fight. Let's go to sleep!''

"You led him on! I saw the way you looked at him!''

"I was only doing what the Generalissimo was doing.''

"Were you ever!''

"Ah, honey, we were just dancing the Rumba. The Rumba doesn't mean anything, it is just a dance.''

"You call that dancing! I call that —'' he told me what he called it. He was furious all over again. "I should have blown his goddamned head off! You fell for him, didn't you?''

Why on earth would Donald think I would fall for a ruffian? Would he keep up this tirade all night? I was so tired, so exhausted. How could I put an end to it? I said, "What a day! And now the man I love is mad with me and wants to fight.''

He was quiet for a moment, then he said he wasn't mad and he didn't want to fight.

"Then, get in your upper bunk and go to sleep.''

He said no.

What a day!

"Donald, His Majesty King Edward VIII will not

like what you have in mind aboard His battleship *Scarborough*.''

Morning came too soon and I was loathe to leave this sudden return to civilization. But just before dawn our washed and dried flying suits were returned to us. Simon was brought from the beach and made fast astern where he bobbled merrily in a brisk trade wind off his starboard quarter. After a breakfast of tea and muffins we went up top side and Donald signed the Ship's Log. Then we said

Donald signs the ship's log.

The captain's gig.

goodbye to our rescuers, our elegant hosts. We climbed down the ship's ladder and boarded the Captain's gig, and freshly uniformed sailors transported us to our plane that was spick and span, and refueled with gas and oil from His Majesty's Navy.

Back to our Sky Path! Path to the clouds! Farewell to the dashing Captain of His Majesty's Navy! Farewell! Good Health! Thank Ye! We swooped and dipped a stiff salute to His Majesty's Ship *Scarborough* and were on our way.

Ministry of Defense
Navy History Branch   22 August 1977
Space 2-E-U
Old War Office Building
Whitehall
London S.W.I.A.
GREAT BRITAIN

Sirs:

In October, 1931 a ship of His Majesty's Navy was in the Caribbean Sea off the coast of British Honduras near Belize. It rescued us when we were downed at nightfall in a flying boat. Would it be possible for you to furnish me with the name of the vessel together with the name of its then Captain?

On the above date the amphibion "Simon Bolivar" of the Latin American Expedition was forced down on the Caribbean off the coast of Honduras. We four aboard the flying boat probably owe our lives to the assistance rendered by a vessel of the Royal Navy.

I am compiling a documentary of the "FLIGHT OF THE LATIN AMERICAN EXPEDITION" but cannot verify the name of the vessel nor its Captain—that portion of my notes and diary have been lost. However, the name of the vessel was similar to "H.M.S. SCARBOROUGH." The name of its Captain is completely lost.

I will be most indebted to you if you can furnish me with the correct name of the vessel together with that of its Captain. All of us are forever grateful for the great aid rendered us by the Royal Navy at that time.

Most sincerely,

Donald C. Beatty.

D. C. Beatty,
F.R.G.S.—1934.

DCB/mc

NAVAL HISTORICAL BRANCH
MINISTRY OF DEFENSE
Empress State Building London SW61TR

Telephone 01-385 1244 ext

Your reference

D. C. Beatty FRGS Esq.   **Our reference**
2800 Overhill Road   D/NHL/1/4/2
Birmingham
Alabama 35223   **Date**
USA   5 September 1977

Dear Sir

Thank you for your letter dated 22 August 1977. HMS Scarborough (Commander A. W. S. Agar, VC, DSO, RN) departed Kingston, Jamaica on 22 October and arrived at Belize, which had recently been devastated by a hurricane on 25 October 1931. Full details of her activities will appear in her Commanding Officer's Report of Proceedings for the period; in common with other naval records of that time, the "ROP" will be held by the Public Record Office, Chancery Lane, London WC2.

It may be of interest that Captain Augustus Agar wrote an extremely entertaining autobiography—*Footprints in the Sea* (Evans Bros., London 1959). In this you will find no account of your incident, but reference to an aircraft accident at New Bedford, Mass, in 1932, in which *he* nearly lost his life.

Yours faithfully,

J. D. B.

1ST Class

Your reference *your letter dated 14/11/77*

Date
23 Nov. 1977

Dear Sir:—

Thank you for your letter postmarked 14 Nov. 1977, from Birmingham, Alabama U.S.A.

Unfortunately, due to our very limited resources, we are unable to conduct this interesting research for you. In the long term, it would be in your best interests **economically**, and would be **more expeditious**, for you, to employ a private professional agent, and I list 3 overleaf .

Yours faithfully,

F. F. Lambert
Kew Search

Public Record Office
Chancery Lane
London WC2
ENGLAND

Sirs:

J. D. Brown, Esq. of the Naval Historical Branch, Ministry of Defense, London informs me that your office is custodian of Royal Navy documents including "Commanding Officer's Report of Proceedings." The specific ROP in which I am interested is said to recite data concerning the HMS *Scarborough* (Commander A. W. S. Agar, VC, DSO, RN) that departed Kingston, Jamaica on 22 October and arrived Belize, which had recently been devastated by a hurricane, on 25 October 1931.

Due to this hurricane, our flying boat, *Simon Bolivar* of the Latin American Expedition, was forced down at nightfall on the Caribbean near Belize. We four aboard the aircraft probably owe our lives to the prompt aid given us by HMS *Scarborough.*

Should there be mention of the assistance rendered us by HMS *Scarborough* in the Commanding Officer's Report of Proceedings, I would be most grateful if you could send me a copy of such mention to further document our unfortunate "ditching" off Belize. And if there is mention of this incident in the ROP I request permission to include it in the records and artifacts of the Latin American Expedition which are permanently housed in the Smithsonian Institution at Washington, D.C. U.S.A.

I look forward with pleasure to receiving your reply.

Respectfully,

D. C. Beatty
FRGS-1935

Public Record Office
Kew, Richmond
Surrey
TW9 4DU

M.A. Beatty, Esq.
2800 Overhill Road
Birmingham
Ala. 35223 *U.S.A.*

Ref: *Q-237*

24 January 1978

Dear Sir

Thank you for your letter dated 30 December 1977, concerning the report of Proceedings of Captain A. W. S. Agar, V. C., R. N.

The log of HMS *Scarborough,* for October 1931, contains many references to the hurricane which struck Belize later that month. No reference is made to an aircraft in distress (reference: *Admiralty: Ships Logs*: 1799-1949: ADM 53/84070).

Admiralty: Admiralty and Secretariat: Cases: 1852-1953: (reference Cases 2924 and 2315 of Admiralty 116/2833) contains the letters of Proceedings No. 8, dated 10 January 1932 from the Commander of HMS *Scarborough* dated 27 November 1931, from Kingston, Jamaica. Para. 8 of Case 2315 states:

"*Scarborough* sailed for Stann Creek at 1200 Wednesday 4 November. Assistance was given to an American Flying Boat (N.R. 182 M) which had landed at dusk and had difficulty finding a suitable beach. This flying boat belonged to the Latin American Expedition to Ecuador and was on her way to the Panama Canal. As there was no accommodation on shore in the village, I accommodated the party of four for the night. They continued their journey early the next morning".

The log of HMS *Scarborough* for November 1931 merely states:

"Burnt scanlight to assist beaching Sea Plane".

The time is 2000, date 4 November 1931 and the reference is ADM 53/84071.

Yours faithfully

F. F. Lambert
Search Department

FFL/hjcw

THE BUZZARDS OF TELA

Again on our way down the coast of British Honduras, Simon was smoothly airborne, with never a whisper of being so fuel-heavy with King Edward the Eighth's gasoline and oil.

We landed in Tela, Honduras, a very small air station, and there was no evidence that any plane had come this way for many months. It was too early to stop for the night, but I was thankful that it was too late to continue further, and I went to bed before the sun went down.

Was I becoming too weary with this Sky Blazing? Could I indeed hold out? I stuck these questions under the bed, with my shoes, and slept.

The field at Tela was dangerously small and rough. Saplings grew so prolifically that it was almost impossible to keep the landing strip cleared. Before taking off, the men walked over the field, feeling with their shoes for stumps, outcroppings, or holes, as small rodents fled at their approach and an occasional snake slithered away into the bush.

Buzzards circled the field and we struck and killed one on takeoff. Buzzard feathers and buzzard other things plastered my window and Tony could see that we had bent a wing strut, but he believed the wing would hold. So we continued on across the black-green jungles of Honduras, although to kill a buzzard was a bad omen, supposedly the forerunner of a crash.

Green Hell

The Black Mahogany Jungles Of Honduras

I dreaded the flight through Green Hell from Tela over jungles, no longer over sea, for I felt secure over water, knowing that Simon could survive a forced landing, no matter how rough. I had learned to love the way he roared across the breakers, sticking his nose under the whitecaps and rising again to settle in the swells, to wallow in the waves. But we could not survive a good wallow in treetops.

There was no seeing through the matted growth beneath us and I knew that not even a slither-dart of sunshine could reach the soggy ground. Honduras lay impenetrable, armor-clad in mahogany. I reflected that truly we were at the mercy of Simon, who in turn was at the mercy of his one motor, that was at the mercy of the gas supply. We were putting all our eggs in one bucket of gasoline. Lord of Petrol! See us through to San Lorenzo!

As we flew over Green Hell we ran into a violent lightning storm. There probably was thunder also but we could hear nothing but the roar of Simon's motor. How could we know that on such a clear day in Tela the weather would turn on us so suddenly? We never would have headed into such a storm, had we known.

Just ahead of us we watched a lightning bolt strike. We watched a twister bite into the jungles and take a mouthful of mahogany. We watched this twister disappear only to gather itself and with lightning strokes bite again into the jungle, leaving fires behind it.

The clouds were gathering and coming at fantastic swiftness around us in a pincer movement. Donald put Simon into a steep bank; we side-slipped through a narrow tunnel of sunlight and retreated. But the storm followed us in our retreat with a speed almost equal to our own as we raced for safety back to Tela, Honduras.

And it rained! We sat around in silence for there was nothing to talk about. Finally Donald said, "No airline can survive without weather reporting. It should be required by law to use radio. Planes could take off and land blind with radio control."

"Honest, Donald, would you take off or land blind with only a radio clicking?"

He answered, "I sure as hell would."

He could include me out for I never would fly with a pilot who wouldn't stick his head out of the window to see where he was going! Donald, Jack, and Tony spoke of variometers, loading coils, vacuum tubes, but my vocabulary did not include these words. I just sat and watched it rain.

Finally the rain ended as suddenly as it had begun. The sun shone, the buzzards returned, and we took off again for San Lorenzo, the very small emergency gas stop that sat precisely on the dividing line between the "Green Hell" of Honduras and the "Pilot's Graveyard" of Nicaragua.

EERIE — EERIE SAN LORENZO

Follow That Love Call!

San Lorenzo sat sideways on a plateau surrounded by deep black lava canyons. It was little more than a landing strip, and the short runway cut a straight-edge between the over-abundantly fertile jungle soil and the totally sterile volcanic rock. It was as though a cleaver had severed the two worlds, dividing the living from the dead and leaving San Lorenzo a River Styx.

There was no apparent access to San Lorenzo except by air, but who would dare to fly into such a place? And I wondered who in God's world would live here!

We landed in this nowhere land and I was glad to get out and stretch my weary bones for my gas-tank-seat was hard and hot and my muscles ached from having no back rest. Amazing! People did live in San Lorenzo, three people in fact, the air field manager, his wife, and an assistant. All three of them ran to meet us as we landed.

The manager's wife (I have forgotten her name) was a young woman from Virginia, who was totally out of place in this isolated spot. But she had set up her home as graciously as though she were in Richmond itself, with crude native mahogany, huge pottery water jugs, tropical flowers and fruits, and many carefully chosen books. And wild animals! There were antelopes, jaguars, honey bears, monkeys, parrots, all loose and wandering around.

It had been so long since she had seen any woman. We talked and we laughed and she brought strange fruits to eat.

I was afraid of the wild animals coming and going as they pleased, and I gladly gave up my fruit to a screaming monkey who snatched it from my hand. She said, "Don't be afraid, they are used to people." But I was afraid, for I certainly was not used to them.

I could not resist asking her, "How on earth did you get here! What in heaven's name made you come!" She told me how her husband had been in the diplomatic service, how his political party lost in the last overthrow of government, and how he elected to sit it out in San Lorenzo in hopes of a return to power with the next overthrow of government. She had preferred to remain with him rather than return to Richmond.

She said, laughing, "And how on earth did you get here? What in heaven's name made you come?" But she knew the answer without my telling her, for my answer was the same as hers, only with slight variations as to circumstances. And we marveled at this thing called LOVE.

I asked, "How did you get that nasty wound down your leg? It looks as though a tiger clawed you."

"It was an antelope, but it was an accident." She defended her pet. "I was trying to carry him, for I had carried him ever since he showed up, half starved, as a baby. He caught me with a hoof." She reflected, "He will be going back to the jungles soon for he is old enough. They always leave when they hear that distant love call."

"Follow that love call!" We both laughed for we knew that we ourselves should have been more ladylike, more civilized than to have followed a love call into these jungles.

She said, taking quinine against malaria as she spoke and offering me some, "Don't be frightened in the night if you hear animals prowling. The doors and windows are barred; they can't get in. Besides, it's not the big things that kill you; it's the little things like mosquitoes."

We talked into the night, sitting under a large tent-like mosquito net. We talked of Richmond, Birmingham, churches and teas, not of revolutions, planes, jungles, or mosquitoes.

It was a most magnificently eerie night, for the moon was full and moonlight was flooding the black volcanoes and casting long witchcraft shadows. Some jungle animals had gone to sleep while others were just awakening and were screaming their weird love calls. But I was so exhausted. Morning would come and we would go. So reluctantly it was off to bed for me.

About midnight I was awakened by the unmistakable sound of cushioned paws under my window. I called to Donald, but he was not there. I was alone. I waited a minute hoping that the cushioned paws would turn and go back to the jungles, but they did not. I listened to the soft crunch of leaves as the prowler came stealthily on to the door of the cabin. I listened intently, then I raised myself on my elbow and held my breath to better hear. I was frozen as I heard the soft creeping paws coming. On and on they came until they reached the door. The door rattled slightly and I knew it would open. I screamed as the door swung open and Donald, in the flooding moonlight, stood startled on the threshold.

"It's you! I thought it was a wild animal."

My stupid husband made a horrible face at me and said, "I am a wild animal!" He took a flying leap into bed, grabbed me, and I felt his teeth on my throat as the bed fell down.

It took a long time to get over my shock and I do not

remember exactly what happened for everything blacked out. But I distinctly remember that way off in the far away he was saying he was sorry—so sorry—so sorry. And I remember most distinctly that I really truly wanted to kill him.

He said, close to my ear, "Promise me something."

"Why should I? I am not so sure I like you."

He said, "Promise me something."

"I am not speaking to you!"

"Promise me something."

"What?"

"That you will never go back to Cuba."

I said I would make him a deal. "You get up and put this bed together, then get in it and go to sleep and I will not go back to Cuba." He said he would get up and put the bed back together.

Again morning came too soon, and again, just before daylight we said farewell to our hosts in San Lorenzo. She said, in parting, in faked Southern drawl, "Pleased to have metcha."

"Thanks, honey child. Pleased to have metcha likewise."

We laughed and kissed goodbye.

What would happen to this girl from Virginia? What would happen to me, for that matter? The same thing would happen to both of us. We would continue to "follow that love call."

PILOT'S GRAVEYARD

There were bad tales about down drafts and cyclonic currents of volcanic Nicaragua. Many pilots who flew into them never came back to report what they had experienced. But we took off and aimed straight for the winds that stormed at us from the volcanoes.

We flew over black mountain peaks ravaged by the storms of time, and beneath us rivers swollen beyond their confines tumbled their violent way to the sea. The continental divide stood stark and splitting and in the distance San Miguel streaked the morning sky with smoke that belched from his crater. Nicaragua moved from the horizon and sprawled black and naked beneath us.

Wind whirlpools caught us and sucked us down toward the lava depths, and we strapped ourselves tighter and held onto the cabin as best we could to keep from being injured; but all of us were sorely bruised before we reached quiet air.

The black-hot air was thick with smoke and permeated with the smell of sulphur and hot lava. The whole scenery seemed a Flo Ziegfeld Extravaganza, designed for an Amsterdam Theatre Ziegfeld Follies Inferno.

Simon lurched and bucked and tried to roll away from it all, and I was glad that Donald was a strong man for it took strength to control a flying boat in this sky.

HER BLACK MAJESTY MOMOTOMBO

Towering in the distance was Momotombo, the largest active volcano in Nicaragua. There she sat, just as Flo Ziegfeld would have designed. Her black majesty held her head high. She was crowned in smoke and robed in lava that scalloped around her and lay in a court train at the foot of her throne. Did red-hot demons guard her domain?

As we flew nearer and nearer, adventure melted into peril, and I knew without being told that we would see into the crater of this active volcano. And by the excitement of the men, I knew that this adventure had been mapped for us before we left New York City. We would get a good look and, hopefully, good pictures of the molten lava of Momotombo. Most probably no man ever had seen this before, for indeed how could a man ever have been so close as we were? But I felt no need to fly into the crater of an active volcano!

The still stronger smell of sulphur and hot lava warned us of our trespassing and the air became even more turbulent. We shot straight up in the smoking current and Donald tried again and again to hold the nose down as we circled on the rim of the crater. At last we corkscrewed

Flying toward the active volcano.

Momotombo

towards the brimstone cone and got a look at earth in the making.

My camera clicked as I tried to hold a focus, but we knew that nothing but smoke would be on the film. Then, with a scorching blast, we were slung high into the sky. The men laughed and saluted as we looked back. Would Momotombo throw rocks at us as we retreated?

One more circle, with cameras grinding, then we landed on Lake Managua, where "The United States Marines had the situation well in hand."

COSTA RICA
WHIP TALK

Behind us and done with were the black volcanoes. Before us was an ocean more beautiful than the Atlantic or the Caribbean. The waters of the Pacific rolled calmly in deep blue.

As usual, we were out of gas!

I watched from my window as we approached for a landing in the surf at Puenta Arenas, a village on a green peninsula. Simon skimmed the surface of the water, seemingly reluctant to settle, preferring to scratch his hot belly in the placid balm. There was no way to bring him out of the water and there was no gas dock, only a half-sunken barge with jagged, twisted sides. So Tony called for a small boat to bring us "gasolina" in five-gallon tins. He called again and again, in his big strong voice, cupping his hands for megaphone. But no boat came. We sat in the sun-heat more than an hour, evaporating precious flying time.

Half-black people, screaming and hallooing, gathered at the water's edge. We knew they heard, we knew they understood, but sullenly they refused to answer.

99

The sullen mob.

One of us had to go ashore in search of fuel, so slowly and gingerly Donald nudged Simon along in the uncertain waters and, inch by inch, approached the half-sunken barge. It took the three of them to fend off from the twisted steel wreck, so I was the one to go ashore. The men questioned the wisdom of my going, but there was no alternative. So Donald boosted me onto the barge. Immediately the half-blacks swarmed around me. They stepped on my feet. One tall boy stepped on the heel of my shoe and pulled it off. They laughed uproariously while I stopped to put it on again and tie it tightly. They pulled at my flying suit. They snatched at my helmet. I tightened it, for I had learned the hard way not to show my long blond hair.

I heard the engine roar for takeoff and I watched until Simon settled in a river away from danger. At least one

hazard had been hurdled. But it was for me to find aero gasoline and I asked for it with every step, "Aero gasolina? Aero gasolina?"

Strangely, I was not afraid, although the mob was constantly growing around me, screaming and pulling at me. Somehow I was through with fear. Certainly I was not impervious to harm, but I had ceased to be impressed by danger. Could one become *blase* to danger, just as one became *blase* to worldly pleasures? No, the word was not *blase*, the word was *bored*. I was just bored with danger and peril, for I had had too much of it. And, also, it was just too much trouble to be afraid.

"Aero gasolina? Aero gasolina?"

At last, the answer came, "Si, Senorita. Si, aero gasolina."

I explained as best I could that we were in a great hurry, and if there was no gasolina in Puenta Arenas, we

Simon hung on the hook while we sat on the wings and fried in the heat.

would continue on to San Jose for it. Much to my relief I was answered in English:

"Senora, of course we have aero gasolina. We supply San Jose with it!" He would service us at once.

A small boat carried me out to the mouth of the river where Simon swung at anchor, and the four of us sat on the wing and waited. I rolled up my pant legs to let my feet hang in the water, but the water was full of sharks that cruised close to Simon, often touching a pontoon. The day boiled and we sat and fried in the heat.

Every few minutes a boy in a small boat would plow through the sharks to tell us that aero gasolina was on its way. After all afternoon of this he came, admitting that they had none, but they would have some next week, if the tanker came. They had something which was just as good and cost only a dollar a gallon. He brought a can of it for us to see. We had wasted so much time! Should we consider taking on this Costa Rican Concoction?

Donald said, "Taste it." He stuck his finger in the can and tasted it. It did not taste like gasoline. Jack and Tony tasted it, "Kerosene?" Tony said, "Pour a spot of it—strike a match." Again and again Tony threw lighted matches at the spot of Costa Rican Concoction. It did not explode, it did not detonate, it did not burn. It only put out the matches. It was not gasoline.

We carried a container of concentrated tetraethyl for an emergency, and now was the time to use it. We put in our tanks thirty-one gallons of Costa Rican Concoction, all they had. With our tetraethyl and luck we might make David, in southwest Panama, before night. But it took them two hours to put in the thirty-one gallons. It was too late to take off.

In a smoldering range Donald brought Simon ashore and staked him down on the river mud bank while the molesters poked and jabbed at the wings. They climbed up on the cabin reaching through the windows to pull at the controls. I sat on the hatch cover to guard the cabin while the men guarded the wings and tail assembly. I sat, trying to fend off, with my feet, the young black boys who were determined to break through and get at the controls. Then I saw a tall white man hurrying through the field towards us, and as he approached the mob quieted down and moved back to let him pass. Donald jumped down from the wing he was guarding to greet him. Tony and Jack joined them and the four men talked for a long time as the mob stood silently by. The tall man said, "You need whips, not guns, to guard you. You need fouets, whip talk. That is what these people understand, whip talk. I will send for guards." He spoke in Spanish to a big black man beside him who replied respectfully, "Si, Father." Then a dozen or more black men echoed, "Si, Father." They bowed slightly and took off in a trot.

"Father to all these!" I was shocked.

Donald chuckled a bit. "Priest, sweetheart, Priest."

He didn't look like a priest to me. There he stood, in an open, unbuttoned, faded blue pajama top, English walking shorts and worn out sandles. His fiery red hair covered his head, most of his face and all of his chest. He gave me a Fatherly smile. But I still didn't believe he was a priest.

The guards came with the longest whips I ever had seen. These men, like vaudeville performers, demonstrated their skill to the cheering crowd as they flipped small objects from great distances with the raw hide of their *fouets*. But before they came the molesters succeeded in breaking two ribs in Simon's wing. Donald, Jack and Tony debated what to do for the night. Surely the guards could not control the mob when the sun went down and it was dark. They decided to put Simon back in the muddy river and anchor where it would be difficult to reach. So they did. And Donald tied two kerosene lanterns to the wings and lit them so that molesters would be seen, if they came. I feared that the lanterns would set Simon afire but Donald said they wouldn't, for he had tied them as galley stoves are tied, so that the boat rocks beneath them while the lanterns remain level and steady. It was a chance we had to take. Besides, the Costa Rican Concoction they called gasolina would not burn. We had tried to burn it with a match and all it did was drown out the match flame. Day was over. Sun was down and we left Simon in the hands of "Whip Talk."

There was a hotel in Puenta Arenas. It had a bathtub. We put up there for three days while the men repaired the damage done to Simon by the mob that had gathered together against us. On the fourth day, after repairs were completed and we were ready to take off, the proprietor of the hotel presented us with a bill equal to that of the Waldorf-Astoria, or even more, and there was nothing we could do about it but pay. All in all it was a most infuriating experience. When the tide came in we left Costa Rica, hopefully forever.

HOTEL CONTINENTAL—
DAVID PANAMA

We sat jittery, wondering if Simon would accept the kerosene put in the gas tank at Puenta Arenas. He would not. Roaring more than was his custom, he spewed out grease and oil and slung it everywhere, over the wings, the fuselage, the windows, until it was almost impossible to see through the windshield. And we knew from the sputtering that he was out of gas, that he would konk, that we were coming down. But where would we land! There was no river, no lake, only jungles. Would we "belly land" in the treetops?

Jack began to crank down the landing gear, but the wheels jammed, halfway down, halfway up, spread eagle. Both Donald and Jack jerked and strained against the controls but the cables were tightly locked; the landing gear would not lower for a wheel landing, neither would it retract for a "belly landing." We could only crash to a stop.

Tony grabbed a small ax and tore away the floorboard in an attempt to reach the controls of the landing gear. He flung pieces of plywood on top of me as he frantically wrecked his way into the hull, and the jagged edges

The wheels jammed half up-half down. We could only crash to a landing.

ripped my arms and cheeks and cut my forehead. Blood! Just what I needed!

He screamed that he had reached the bicycle chain that had slipped off the sprockets and jammed the controls; he could almost reach it with his hand. "PUSH-A ME INTO THE HULL!" he yelled. And I put my feet against his bottom and pushed with all my might. With splitting of plywood and tearing of leather his shoulders disappeared under the floorboard, halfway into the hull, and he screamed, "I'VE GOT IT!"

With his wriggling and my pushing, he seemed to be slipping into the hull, and I debated holding to his legs to prevent it. But my weight against his would be nothing and there was no reason for both of us to fall through. So I sat and did nothing. Somehow I was not frightened, although this was my first crash. I was only annoyed, and I longed for the peace and quiet I had known in Birmingham. (This was when I reached for my Brownie camera and took a picture of the wheel that stuck, spread-eagle, beside my window.) With a last sputter Simon gasped, dropped his too heavy nose straight towards the jungle, and konked. All was silence. Down we came. Then Jack screamed, pointing wildly, "DAVID!"

Lady Luck just one more time. Wheels, wheels, please wheels! She heard it, for with a sudden jolt, the wheels dropped into place inches off the ground and we bumped and bounced merrily across the landing field, then ground looped to a stop.

It was early in the afternoon when we landed, but the men had no appetite for inspection, no appetite for plotting tomorrow's course, nor for seeking aero gasoline. It was time to quit for the day. This had been the closest call we had had and all four of us were unnerved. I for one was going to bed, and I was going to stay there. This perpetual commotion was beginning to be bothersome.

The hotel was strange. The large sign over the white frame one-story building read, HOTEL CONTINEN-TAL—DAVID PANAMA. It was not my idea of a hotel, for there were no rooms, no doors, no locks. It was only a bunk house, a dormitory with alcoves for beds. Wooden partitions between the alcoves extended up to six feet, and all one had to do to see, and to know all about his next bed sleeping companion, was to stand on the splitbottom chair and look over the partition. There was no one in the hotel but me when I went to bed, for I stood on the splitbottom chair and looked to see.

All the beds were empty, some unmade. A large wire-framed, tent-like mosquito net hung against the ceiling, directly over each bed, and a crank, attached to the wall, lowered it into place. One knew by the squeaking of the rusty crank that the next bed sleeping companion was retiring for the night.

I cranked down my mosquito net and found that the frame was much larger than the bed, and it lay copiously on the floor, so I need not worry about touching it during the night. If I slept in the middle of the bed mosquitoes could not reach through the holes to bite. Then I pumped

vigorously with a Flit-gun inside the net, and oily mist settled on the bed sheet, bringing with it a black pepper
sprinkling of dead mosquitoes. I shook them off onto the
floor and they fell across a procession of teeny little red
ants that crossed, in a waving line, the wide wooden plank-
ing. (These were the smallest ants I ever had seen.) Then I
climbed into bed, ducking under my net, with my ears still
aching, and I choken on Flit vapor.

In a few minutes I heard the squeaking crank at the
end of the hotel and I wondered who else was going to bed
so early, probably Jack or Tony. But I could tell by the
coughing that it was a big fat man who smoked crude
tobacco and drank cerveza national (beer). He was either
as tired as I was or else he was drunk, for immediately he
snored.

For awhile I watched the billions of little red ants that
marched in perfect formation, never deviating from the
path set by those who led the line. Who ever saw so many
ants! Ants! Ants! Then I pulled the too-small bed sheet
over my head and tried to go to sleep, but I couldn't sleep
for teeny little red ants stomping through my room.

I lay there remembering San Lorenzo. "It's not the
big thing that kills you, it's the little thing." How true. All
the giants of destruction Simon could handle, like hurricanes and volcanoes. But the little thing would kill him, a
little thing like a bucket of gasoline setting quietly and
silently, just out of his reach. Who was the God of Petrol?
Jupiter Rex? Neptune? Lady Luck? No, none of these.
When one is out of gas, the God of Death steps in.

I went to sleep and got some rest, even at Hotel Continental. The next morning the men made a complete inspection of Simon. Tony washed away the oil and grease
that splatter-painted everything and he replaced a section
of the floorboard that he had wrecked off to reach the

landing gear controls. Again, we had a small place to put our feet and Simon was completely sound and ready to go.

So on to the Panama Canal! On to Cristobal! But the men were beginning to know that it would be suicidal to fly further south, where landing facilities and refueling would be nonexistent.

But it began to rain. Then it poured, then the ceiling fell out. We sat on the floor of the narrow porch, listening to it pound on the tin roof, watching it gush off the corrugated eaves in broad straight poles. We were imprisoned behind bars of water that flashed when the lightning struck.

Frustration. Boredom. Tony decided to do something drastic, like washing his clothes that hadn't been washed in weeks. It seemed a good idea. All of us would do the same. But Tony was too enthusiastic and washed all he owned, not remembering that nothing would dry until the rain stopped. Then he had nothing dry to wear, not even a bandanna. He put on wet pants. And he muttered "BLOCK-A HEAD!"

Day after day the rain kept coming back, like a cat that won't get lost. Cristobal so close! Should we take off in this weather? Where is the line between chance and suicide? With all the chances we already had taken, dare we take another? Yes. We took off.

We wove a course through the ground clouds, following darting arrows of light that pointed the way. And we climbed above the thick backdrop of rain that screened off the mountains. At last we broke out above the clouds and into the bright sunshine of a tropical morning. But the clouds beneath us blanketed the earth completely and there was no knowing where the ground lay or where the mountains rose.

Little by little the clouds thinned and the wind blew

them away. At long, long last, welcome to the sunshine! Gatun Lake, controlling the waters for the Panama Canal, lay below us in placid tropical sunlight and shadows, and we circled low to see.

Stumps! Stumps! Stumps! Hundreds of them held floating islands of orchid close in their roots, as bobbing channel buoys marked the path between them. Yellow blossoms spilled into the water, a pot of gold at rainbow's end.

The lake lay so quiet, so motionless, so serene. Here there was no violent storm, no raging sea, here there was only a dreamy haven of rest. This Land of Sleeping Beauty! The exquisiteness of the serenity strangely upset me, for I was so weary, so exhausted, so depleted. This safe harbor seemed only for me—for me alone.

A wave of sadness—why were my tears spilling! Lady Luck! DO SOMETHING! Lady Luck, I must not cry!

With a sudden wingover, Simon rose and turned to Calebra Cut, then back again to Gatun Lake. Boats! Boats! Freighters, tankers, sailing vessels, all waiting to go through the locks, for the locks had been closed for two weeks, due to flooding. Never had anyone remembered such rains. Luxury liners from all over the world hung at anchor awaiting dock space.

With another wingover we flew over the Canal Zone and on to France Field, the United States Army Base which was under water by two inches. Simon slipped and slid on the cement water-covered runway, then ground-looped to a stop.

Our clothes were wet. My film was ruined, melted, and stuck together, and we were weary with the antics of Aquarius as we walked to the immigration office to present our passports, our medical certificates, and verification of our permit to fly over the territory of Panama.

At last! Cristobal!

CRISTOBAL—
JOURNEY'S END

Cristobal! Journey's beginning!

The scientists from the Smithsonian and from the United States Navy had arrived two weeks before and were proceeding with their plans for the Great Adventure that lay ahead. The Latin American Expedition would go from Panama on the Pacific to Guayaquil, Ecuador. It would sail by tramp steamer to Guayaquil, when and if one was available. There was no predicting when tramp steamers would sail. From Guayaquil the expedition would continue by mule back, on foot, by dugout, by raft. Who could be sure how they could cross the Andes and reach the Amazon River and the Atlantic coast of Brazil? For this 2300 mile trek was through territory marked on maps simply as UNEXPLORED. The men were packing with utmost care, for it would take eight months, or longer, before they made contact with the outside world.

Cristobal. Journey's End.

Journey's end for Jack. He booked first available passage by luxury liner back to Broadway and Bright Lights. Jack had had enough. He wanted no more.

Journey's end for Tony and Simon. They would be

111

returned to New York City's Roosevelt Field, from whence they came. Pilot E. K. Jaquith would be employed to fly them back.

And Journey's End for me. I would return by Standard Fruit Boat to New Orleans, then by train, the Humming Bird, to Birmingham, Alabama—Home.

I watched as Jacquith, not knowing Simon, roughly forced him onto the step and yanked him off the water. With blurring eyes I watched him climb and head due north as he became smaller and smaller and as his thundering voice grew dim. Then he disappeared beyond the horizon and all was quiet.

I wept when I heard that, for no apparent reason at all, Simon split to pieces in the sky, fell and sank into the sea. Sailors aboard the American freighter, *Henry S. Groves*, spotted the splash and, with full speed ahead, reached the scene and hauled from the waves the near-death Tony and Jaquith. But Davy Jones had claimed for his own *Simon Bolivar*.

It was a sad night for me when I said goodbye to the man I loved and sailed home, alone—in the rain.

WINGS ACROSS

THE HIGH ANDES

It was an empty trip home, a time containing nothing. After the first three days, however, I began to think of home, especially of my baby, Madelyn. It was the first time I ever had been separated from her, and I remembered how hard it is to kiss a baby goodbye.

Each day became longer, but at last, New Orleans! Where the Rebel Flag flies high!

Small tugboats chugged joyously out to meet us. They nudged us along with their plaited hemp rope bumpers, holding us securely in the channel that led to the

dock. Big black men caught hawsers and snubbed us up tight to the pier, and the gangplank reached out to grab a toehold.

There in all the noise and bustle of docking was my father! He stood away from the crowd, waving both his arms over his head so that I would spot him. He really had come all the way to New Orleans to meet me! And my sweet mother, holding my baby in her arms, was waving a long bright colored scarf, so that I would see that she and my baby were there. When I ran down the gangplank my baby squealed and gave me wet all-face kisses. Arms were around me. I was home! And I was almost happy.

It was a long ten months before I heard from Donald, for there was no way I could hear. But one day this long ten months ended, and there was a letter from Iquitos, Amazonas. I grabbed my letter, profusely thanking the postman who delivered it, and I fled to my home to read it, alone. I locked the door behind me so that no one could come in.

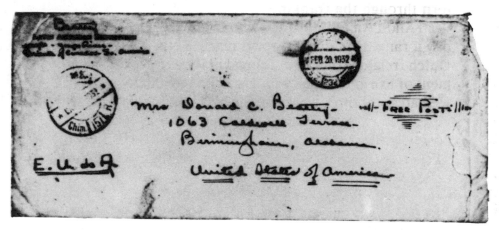

My letter had come to me by runner then by dugout down the Yaupe River to an outpost on the Amazon.

His letter said many things I had not heard for many months. It said all the things I wanted it to say, and it said them over and over again. But above everything, it said that by the time I received it Donald too would be out of the jungles and on his way home.

A Jivaro Indian runner had brought my letter by dugout to the outpost, and from there it had come by many handlings to me. Donald was on a raft when he wrote, and he would come out of the jungles as my letter had come, by dugout to the outpost, from there down the Amazon River to Iquitos, Amazonas. From Iquitos he would catch a once-a-month riverboat to Para, Brazil, and there he would catch some tramp steamer to some port beyond Para. "God knows when the boats will run," he wrote, "for there is no scheduling of such things."

Donald suggested I save the envelope. It might be an interesting one to keep, for my letter had been delivered without stamps. It was franked, in handwriting, by "Donald Croom Beatty, as authorized by the International Postal Union." I was sorry that, in my haste, I had torn through the franking.

And I waited. I waited actually by the telephone. One day it rang. Donald at last had reached N.Y.C. via a small Dutch freighter that had stopped in Para to pick up a shipment of live animals and snakes from the jungles of Brazil. He had spent three weeks on the high seas in this Ark, with its cargo, two of each kind, slated for the Bronx Zoo, hopefully for reproduction. And he loved me—HE LOVED ME—HE LOVED ME—Had the baby received her wild animals?

"No! WHAT WILD ANIMALS!"

He had carefully nursed ten cuddly little baby animals on his raft down the Amazon. He wasn't too sure what they were, but he had shipped them to Madelyn for her third birthday present. They should have arrived long before now. And he loved me—"What WILD ANIMALS! What will I do with them?"

He would be home in a few days. There was Expedition business to complete before he could leave New York City.

Madelyn's animals arrived before Donald. They were not adorable and cuddly, as he said they were. They were fierce, snarling, hissing jungle beasts that had outgrown their cages during the weeks in transit. One of them clawed a bloody gash in my arm when I went too close to his cage, trying to see what sort of animal he was, and my father rushed me to Doctor Beddow who gave me a tetanus shot and sewed me up. Then my father had Madelyn's animals recaged into larger confines in his rose garden, for there was no other place for them.

Worse, some of Madelyn's animals slept by day while others slept by night, so in our house no one slept any time at all, for jungle beasts were screaming and fighting to get out and eat each other. My three-year-old daughter was ecstatic over her wild animals. "I want to watch him eat him!" she screamed in glee. My father was furious, so was my mother, so was I. So were all the neighbors, who called the police and the fire department to settle the disturbance.

Donald and not I would have to tell Madelyn that her jungle animals had to go to the Avondale Zoo.

My father observed, caustically, "Donald can't be far behind."

Happy times! Donald arrived! All the family was at the Terminal Station to meet him. He was tan and slim, lithe and muscular. A man just out of the jungles.

These were not times to relate to a diary.

Honors came to Donald for his accomplishments. He was made a fellow of the Royal Geographic Society, and he was elected into membership of the prestigious Explorers Club. But his main interest and concern was in his findings from Amazona, for this data must be put into permanent records.

This was the hardest time of all for us, for every detail of his findings pointed clearly and unequivocally to the fact that no airline could operate through this impenetrable land. The Latin American Expedition only proved, without a doubt, that Amazonas was not ready for aviation and aviation was not ready for Amazonas.

Donald Croom Beatty—from the jungles, back to civilization.

ASSEMBLY BASE AT QUENCA, ECUADOR

Pablo with his mud covered muleteers and cargodores with 27 pack animals finally arrived from Mendez—animals too tired to rub noses or to whinny were standing around with drooped heads and wide spread feet. Our cargo was loaded immediately for the long trec across the westernmost cordillera and we left at first light of day, before the rain started, for it only requires a little rain to make the trail impassible. We were at high altitude and in the clouds all day. Everything was wet—cold. . . Pablo said would we please proceed as quietly as possible because the rain resulted in a sudden or loud noise.

The narrow trail, fifteen inches wide in spots and wet as could be, was constantly giving away under foot. One pack mule, with valuable equipment, was lost over a cliff.

Seven weeks of walking over the Andes with pack teams.

Jivaro selects prime balsa wood for rafts for the long journey to the Amazon. Who could know how long?

ON THE BANKS OF THE RIO UPANO
Latitude 3°

Jivaro selects sturdy wood for cages for live animals. These cages will be lashed to the rafts and the animals will be eaten along the way.

TSANTSA

A warrior holds the shrunken human head over a pot of boiling water. After the features are softened, the eyes and lips will be sewn together and the features will be molded into permanent form between the thumb and forefinger of the warrior.

The ritual is over. The powers of the victim have been transferred to the victor. The head has no further value for the Tsantsa has been completed.

Jivaro warrior proudly displays weapon acquired by trading his blowgun and poison darts.

Warrior's wife number one proudly displays necklace of beads traded for her dancing belt of snail shells.

Expedition:

Organized and directed Latin American Expedition of 1931/32. This expedition departed from the U.S. on September 26th, 1932 and returned in May '32. The field of operation took in the southwest portion of the Oriente of Ecuador and a small corner of northeast Peru.

General assembly base had been established at Cuenca, Ecuador to prepare for packtrain trip across the second cordillera of the Andes to Mendez at Latitude 3°-5'S., Long. 78°-35'W. A camp at this point was made to prepare for trek on foot with carriers over the westernmost cordiller and into the indian county of the Oriente.

Departing Mendez, a trail was set in a northern direction to the Rio Patusa and then north again to where the Rio Tagacu joins the Upano at Lat. 2°-50'S., 77°-45'W. Leaving the Mangostra, a winding southwest course was taken to the junction of the Kanga with the Rio Upano at L. 3°-30'S., L78°-50'W. A three weeks "rest" camp was established at this point, during which motion pictures were made of the Jivaro indians.

Leaving the junction of these rivers by balsa rafts and canoes, the course taken being down the Upano to the rio Santiago. The course of the Santiago was then followed to its mouth in the rio Maranon. The unexplored territory between the Santiago and Marona rivers had been explored during the course down the Santiago as well as plane table work on the Santiago river. The Santiago and Morona empty into the Maralon at 77°-35'W., 4°-25'S., and 77°-5'W.,, 4°-45'S; one above, the other below the Pongo Mansiriche.

Once upon the waters of the Maranon this stream was followed, with occasional deviations for exploration along its banks until Iquitos, Peru was reached. From Iquitos we "backtracked" to 77°-35'W., 4°-25' S., and using seaplanes conducted flights of the unexplored territory between the rivers Santiago, Marona and Pastaza.

Motion and still pictures of the life of the Jivaro indians, their ceremonies and mode of living were made throughout the above. Celestial observations and plane table work were also made.

From Iquitos the organization proceeded by river steamer to Para at the mouth of the Amazon and from there back to the U.S.

It is contemplated that certain parts of the above territory will be more thoroughly investigated by the undersigned sometime in the near future.

Donald and I were devastated. For us, three years and all we had were worse than wasted. And now the best we could hope for was to be able to roll with the blow and begin all over again with something else.

Donald cloistered himself in his room, referring to his field notes and to his memory, and his typewriter clicked away for endless hours.

One morning, while his typewriter clicked, the phone rang. It was long distance from N.Y.C. for Donald. Mr. MacGregor, president of the newly formed Pan American Grace International Airlines in South America, was on the phone. He and Donald talked for a long time and, after the conversation ended, Donald said to me, "Sweetheart, would you like to go to Chile—tomorrow?"

He had to be joking, and I laughed because this was silly. He said, "Don't laugh, Sweetheart. I'm not joking.

Would you like to go to Chile tomorrow—for three years—maybe longer?"

Then he related his conversation with Mr. MacGregor. A trimotored Ford of this new airline, Panagra, had disappeared in the High Andes with sixteen passengers and crew. It had been lost for months and all search for it had been unsuccessful. However, this plane, the *San Jose*, had to be found for, according to Chilean law, no person could be pronounced legally dead until found. Therefore the estates of all the passengers and crew were frozen and were hopelessly legally entangled.

An experienced pilot had to be found for this difficult job of search, a pilot qualified to fly multimotored seaplanes and the trimotored Ford; a pilot with a radio license and who spoke both English and Spanish; a pilot who knew the High Andes and who understood high altitude flying; a pilot who would go to Chile for three years, or longer.

I said, "Where would he find such a pilot? There is not a man on earth with all those qualifications."

Silence. Cold, dead, tingling silence. I knew a pilot who was all these things. And he stood before me, churning with conflicting thoughts, as was I.

We talked into the morning, Donald and I. Should we go to Chile? Would we go to Chile? Dare we go to Chile, for three years or more? Mr. MacGregor must know immediately. Would Donald be so kind as to call him tomorrow with his decision?

In the morning Donald called Mr. MacGregor. Yes, we would go. Yes, we would leave at once. Yes, Donald would leave today. Yes, Madelyn and I would leave the following day so that we could catch the next Grace Line steamer out of N.Y.C. to Panama.

Mr. MacGregor said to me, "Mrs. Beatty, if you possibly can manage, would you please take only one suitcase apiece for we have a weight problem in flying from Panama to Santiago, Chile.''

"Yes, I can imagine. I understand maximum weight problems.''

"I heard you understood these things. It is nice to welcome aboard a wife like you.''

It was not a happy departure, for our families were frozen in disbelief. But the departure was so sudden that I had no time to think or to care. But why Chile! Why in heaven's name Chile? Chile, a land far below the equator where it becomes cold and frigid as it approaches the South Pole. Why Chile, when I loved the tropics!

Donald left immediately, within a couple of hours. Madelyn and I left the following day.

Personnel from the Grace Steamship Line met us at the Pennsylvania Station and raced us across N.Y.C. to the docks where the steamer, *Santa Elaina*, was being held for our arrival. The *Santa Elaina* had been held for three hours. The Captain paced the deck; visitors at Bon Voyage parties were goggle-eyed with champagne. Everyone was longing for departure and farewell. Passengers leaned against the rail to watch us climb the gangplank to see what great celebrities were boarding, for who was so great that the Grace Line would hold departure of the *Santa Elaina* for three hours?

Donald saw us coming and came quickly to assist, to carry Madelyn in his arms. Grace Line personnel scurried aboard with our suitcases and stuffed animals. The instant my foot hit the deck the gangplank began to move aweigh and into the hull. It was all very breathless and all very disappointing for the passengers who had good reason to expect more important and more interesting passengers than my little girl and me.

To reach the frozen south one goes thru the dreamy tropics, and the further the *Santa Elaina* plied her way the warmer it became. My baby, Madelyn, adored it all. She ran the decks with me in hot pursuit. She stood on the bow, holding tightly to her daddy's hand while the wind blew salt spray in her face. Happiness shone in her every movement.

We were headed south, across the equator and south as far as transportation could take us, because Santiago, Chile, was the furthermost point, unless one made his own arrangements to continue south to the Polar Regions.

SIKORSKY S-38 "MISS FANCY" AND CAPTAIN STEVE DUNN

Our Grace Line Cruise ended in Panama for at Cristobal, Panama Canal Zone, it was back into the air for us, back into the air flying this exciting new airline, Panagra, all the way to Santiago, four days, maybe five, depending upon the weather.

We were scheduled to fly the first two days of our flight to Santiago, Chile, by Sikorsky S-38 with Captain Steve Dunn as pilot and with Donald as co-pilot. It had been many months since either of us had been in the air and neither of us ever had been on an airline. Airlines were great new things, just the sort of thing Donald wanted for himself. Today was the big day! Today he would fly as co-pilot on this great new international airline, Pan American Grace, "Panagra."

We arrived at France Field before daybreak. The Sikorsky sat in readiness for take-off, chocks under the wheels, mechanics walking around casually. There were no passengers, as usual, for not many people flew; most who traveled preferred the two or three weeks trip by steamer rather than the risk of a three or four days' trip in the sky.

"Donald," I asked, "are you going to take off

without checking this plane? Aren't you going to look it over yourself?''

"Sweetheart, this is an airline. The mechanics check everything. The pilot has nothing to do with checkouts."

"You mean you trust the mechanics? You really are willing to take their word? They stay on the ground, they aren't up there with us. How do you know the gas tanks are full? Aren't you going to stick your finger in to see?''

"Of course I am not going to climb up there and stick my finger in the gas tanks!''

"Ah, honey, I'm afraid to fly, not knowing if the tanks are full!''

I was not pleased with this airline arrangement. But Donald would not climb up on the wing to see if the tanks were full. So I hushed.

Just before daybreak Captain Steve Dunn arrived. He was a most friendly young man, apparently in his late twenties. His pretty wife, Marie, had come to see him off. And also, to bid Captain Dunn farewell, Lorita, the parrot, sat quietly and silently on Captain Dunn's shoulder, like a picture of Long John Silver. Neither Captain Dunn nor his wife, Marie, commented at all about the parrot. It was their custom to bring her to France Field to see the takeoff, for Lorita enjoyed it and always screamed in delight as the Sikorsky roared its way off the field and into the air.

Captain Dunn had bought his parrot in Jamaica and he had taught her to say many things, some of which Mrs. Dunn disapproved. But Lorita, while trained to talk, also had been trained to shut up, which was wise training for a parrot from Jamaica. This morning Lorita was to say only, "Goodbye, sweetheart."

Time came to take off, and Captain Dunn kissed Marie goodbye and transferred Lorita from his shoulder to hers. He said, straight in Lorita's face, "Say goodbye to daddy!'' Lorita said, most distinctly and with a sob, ''Goodbye, sweetheart! Goodbye, sweet, sweet, sweet, sweet, sweet—''

''Lorita! Say sweetheart!''

''Sweetheart!''

''Good girl!''

Madelyn could not believe her ears, for she never had heard a bird talk. She wanted Lorita. She cried for Lorita. She screamed for Lorita. She sat down on the ground, refused to get up without Lorita. I picked her up, screaming and kicking. ''Honey,'' I said, ''if we ever come back to Panama I will buy you a parrot but parrots can't fly in airplanes. It would make them sick. You wouldn't want to make Lorita sick, would you?''

Madelyn continued to scream. Sick or not sick, she wanted Lorita. ''Look, honey, quick! Daddy is getting in the plane! Look quick!''

Instantly Lorita was forgotten as she watched her daddy step on a wheel, throw his leg across the hatch over the pilot's cockpit, step down onto the pilot's seat, and settle into position as co-pilot.

''Why won't they let daddy go in the front door?''

''Honey, they make the passengers go through the door. Only the pilots can climb in the window.''

''I want to climb in the window like daddy!''

Captain Dunn, as had Donald, stepped on the wheel and slung himself through the window and into the left cockpit.

A steward helped us aboard and he brought us cotton balls to stuff in our ears to mute the noise of the engines. And he gave us chewing gum. ''Chew and swallow a lot,'' he said. ''It will keep your ears from popping.'' He added, ''If your ears get to hurting, hold your nose and blow. That will relieve the pressure.'' Mechanics pulled the chokes, the engines revved up, and we moved slowly down the broad cement ramp and into the water. There we lay afloat, engines quietly idling, until the wheels could be removed. The wheels would not be needed on the flight. They would only be useless excess weight, because only water landings were made further south.

Welcome aboard! Happy landings! All the personnel of Panagra wore uniforms.

We watched as two tremendous black men, wearing brief swim trunks, went into the water, one on each side of the Sikorsky. They disappeared under the water beneath the Sikorsky and removed the wheels. Then they surfaced. Each of them rolled a wheel up the broad cement ramp, where a truck lifted the wheels and carried them to storage. The wheels were very heavy because they were filled with water and not air, so that they would sink beneath the seaplane to facilitate removal.

As soon as the wheels were disposed of, the Sikorsky moved away from the docking and out into the deep water. Little by little it edged its way beyond the breakwater, then with a sudden burst of power from both engines, we were on the step and airborne, although I wasn't quite sure when it was, so smooth was the takeoff. Had I ever felt such smoothness! What a pilot! But this was Panagra Airline and this was the great seaplane captain, Captain Steve Dunn.

The Sikorsky amphibian was a beautiful plane. It was battleship gray, inside and out. All the upholstering was red leather and the deck between the seats was carpeted in red. The seats were adjustable (imagine!) and reclining. There was a metal bar for a footrest and there was almost room to stretch one's legs straight out.

Being not only an airplane but also a boat, the Sikorsky carried all the safety equipment required for a seagoing craft. It carried a life raft, with two paddles, two canvas life rings, two canvas dock fenders, several cork life preservers, a flare pistol, hundreds of feet of line, a monkey-fist (for heaving), and a sea anchor. There might have been additional equipment stored in the hull, I do not know. The piece of marine equipment that gave the most trouble, however, was the ship's fog bell that hung directly behind the pilot's cockpit and clanged every time the plane banked. Although against regulations for the sea, the bell

Passenger seat, wheel, flare gun, ship's bell, and life boat paddles (note yardstick) for comfort and safety aboard the Sikorsky S-38.

Yardstick

had to be lashed down and secured, because once it had broken loose, clanged loudly, and frightened passengers. With weight such a critical consideration, I could not understand the requirement of weighing us down with all this equipment that was practically worthless.

There were no passengers today, only Madelyn and me. However the Sikorsky was designed to carry eight passengers, and it carried water and box lunches for them. Would you believe, the Sikorsky had a toilet! I never heard of such a thing! How fancy could you get! It was not called a toilet, it was called THE THRONE.

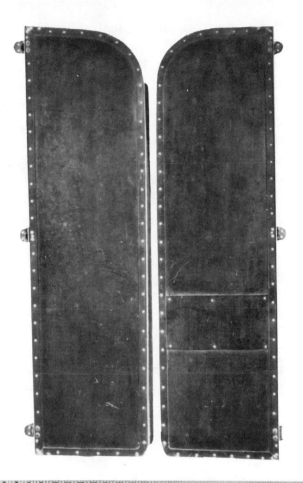

Yardstick

Doors to the throne.

The Throne Room was a very small compartment in the tail section of the plane, in the very back of the passenger cabin. Two small doors, like minature bar doors, partially concealed the passenger who sat upon the Throne. But these doors would not flap closed behind a fat man, for the Throne Room really was not large enough for anyone. And it was the custom for passengers to keep "eyes front."

137

There was nothing mechanical about the Throne. It was a "Chic Sales." One saw straight through it to the ground, or the treetops. And there was a printed card of instruction glued to the wall beside it, like the instruction in a Pullman car toilet, which read, "Passengers will please refrain from using toilet while the plane is standing on the runway."

The sign had a lilt to it and modulated easily into song. It made a great drinking song and when the plane stopped to refuel the pilot and passengers put their arms around each other and sang it with gusto, harmonizing "Barber Shop" to Anton Dvorak's "Humoresque."

Humoresque
(Theme)

Poco lento et gracioso

Anton Dvorak

Pas-sen-gers will please re-frain from | us-ing toi-let while the plane is stand-ing on the run-way I love | You-uo-uo-ou

It had many verses, none of which I will record here.

Our first day's flight from Panama was almost entirely over the Pacific. We maintained an altitude of five hundred feet, which seemed unreasonably high to me, for I loved to fly skimming the water. But this was the altitude prescribed. There were almost no beaches as I had known beaches on the Atlantic or on the Gulf. Those that we flew over were not of white sand but of dark coral. The dark rugged reefs were filled with birds, nesting and feeding along the water line, and the Pacific lay beneath us in quiet purple most of the time. Only occasionally was it rough and frosted with whitecaps.

It was a great first day. Having no passengers, we had this big airliner all to ourselves. With Captain Dunn it was such smooth flying that we took off our seat belts and walked around in the aisle, a thing I had never done and never heard of anyone doing, and Madelyn tossed her stuffed Mickey Mouse and let him hang by his tail from the back of a seat.

Our first docking was at Buenaventura, Colombia. The Sikorsky was carefully placed into position at the foot of a steep hundred-foot-long ramp that led to a mesa-like refueling station atop a sandy hill. Cables were securely fastened to flush-mounted rings in the stem and sides. Guiding cables were hand-held as a hand winch atop the hill carefully guided the Sikorsky up the steep incline.

After refueling and after taking an additional respite to stretch our backs and to let Madelyn run and jump a bit, Captain Dunn called, "ALL ABOARD!" The hand winch and guiding cables lowered the Sikorsky down the steep ramp and we were in the water again.

From this water takeoff we felt no lift into the air, no flinging free from the waves. I did not know exactly when we were airborne. Airline flying was a world apart from all I had known before. This Sikorsky was fancy! Miss Fancy was she!

There were many interesting dockings along our way south, for we stopped several times a day to refuel. The one Madelyn liked best was the one at Tumaco, Colombia, where black naked Indians took her to ride in a dugout while the Sikorsky was being refueled.

The dugout (with, of all things, an outboard motor) was used to handle a floating gangplank for passengers. As we approached Tumaco, we saw the dugout pushing the gangplank away from the dock to make way for the Sikorsky that was coming in for a water landing.

Make way! Make way for Miss Fancy! The Sikorsky landed in the bay, taxied to the floating dock and nosed up onto a floating ramp. When she had been carefully snubbed into place, the dugout came back, towing the gangplank so that passenger could disembark and stretch themselves on the twenty by twenty-four foot, floating-on-empty-gas-drums seaport.

Madelyn was completely fascinated with the dugout, not noticing at all that the Indians wore no clothes. She wanted to ride in the dugout. She screamed to ride in the dugout. She lay down on the dock, refused to get up.

Captain Dunn said, "Take the kid to ride. Make it snappy. It is getting late."

Panagra airport on the Equator, Tumaco, Colombia.

Beautiful ladies brought luscious fruits. (Photo taken from atop Sikorsky engine.)

Another dugout pushed off shore and paddled to the floating gas dock bringing with it the most tremendous fruits. The bananas were more than a foot long. The paltas were as large as cantaloupes. Melons were of many varieties, huge and beautiful.

We could carry none of this luscious fruit with us, for we were at maximum weight with gasoline for the long flight across the Pacific to Selinas. And it would be a long time before we ate again. So we ate all we could and left the rest to rot in the tropical sun.

Tumaco is just north of the Equator and Selinas is just south of it. So we had a rare treat ahead of us, Madelyn and I. Neither of us had ever crossed the Equator. Captain Dunn said, "Donald, would you like to fly your family over the Equator?" Donald said, "I sure as hell would!"

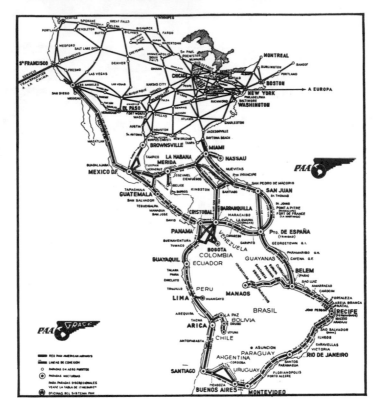

—from the records of Harold R. Harris, founder of Panagra.

Making a survey of how to start an airline in South America in 1927, I traveled by surface means the only way then: steamer, New York to Panama, Columbia, Ecuador, Peru. Railroad from Peru to Lake Titicaca. Steamer across the lake to Bolivia, and railroad to Argentina. Then steamer to Uruguay and Brazil and back to New York. An airline pilot's dream?

In 1928 the Pan American Airways group and W. R. Grace Company put up the money to get the dreamed airline started, and the first section was in operation on September 13, 1928—the first American flag airline in the world south of the Equator.

A half century later we find that not only our flag, but the flags of all the nations concerned are on airlines covering the great distance required to tie the entire globe together.

This happened not because of some fancy legislation in some world capitol, but by the hard, dedicated work of many individuals, most of them unknown, whose stories will be forgotten.

However, here we have some details of one family that helped to make this dream come true.

A map of the Panagra air routes in South America follows.

142

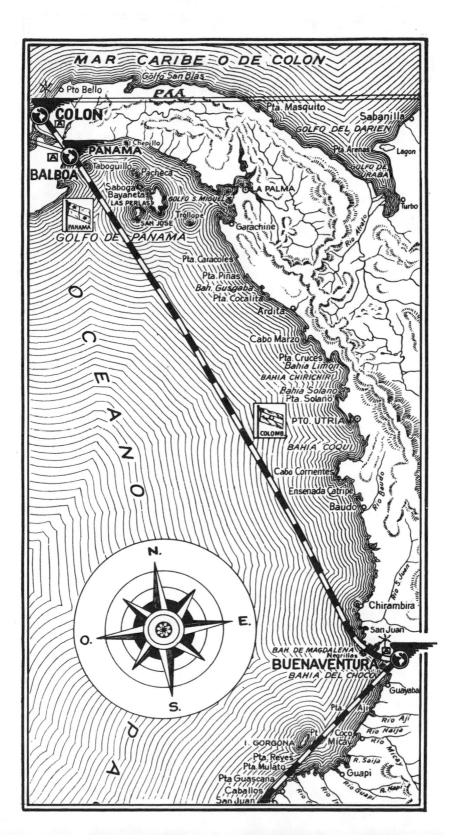

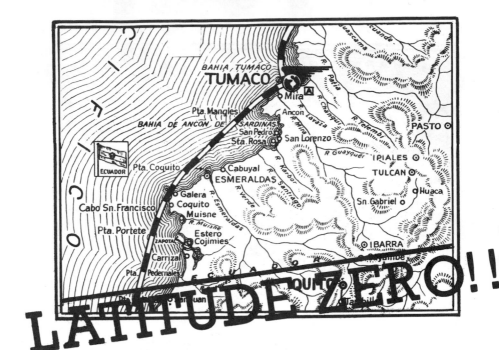

LATITUDE ZERO! Earth's equator! The Realms of His Exalted Majesty, Mighty God of the Sea, Neptune! LATITUDE ZERO! Today, this morning, in the equatorial sun, I would cross the equator for the first time. I would bow in humble obedience to the God of the Sea. What was going to happen to me?

I heard tall tales of torture inflicted upon those who crossed for the first time. Aboard steamship, one is flung into the briny swimming pool, wearing one's best evening gown. Or one is smeared with grease that will not wash off for days. Or one's hair is cut off and flung into the waves, to appease His Mighty Majesty, Neptune.

But what, in the air, in the Realms of Jupiter Rex, God of Sky? Would Jupiter Rex not come to my defense when I was in his realm? Captain Dunn and Donald had crossed many times and they were immune. But my baby and I were not. In the air, surely we could not be flung into the briny deep, not smeared with grease. Nor could we have our tresses cut. Donald would not dare!

I was glad that Donald was to fly us across the

144

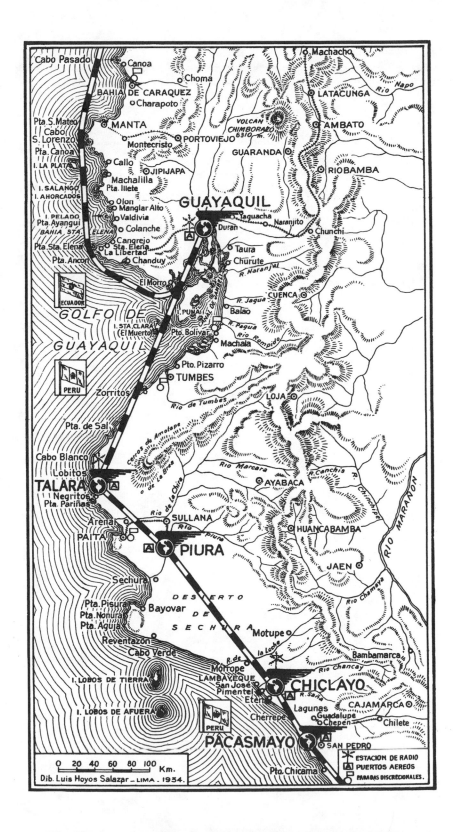

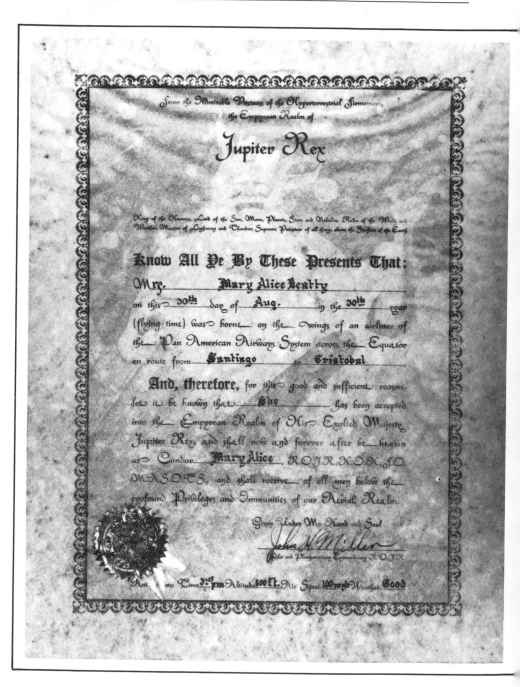

Equator, for I had known Captain Dunn but for a day. I was not too sure of his sense of humor. In fact I was not too sure of his ability as a pilot. I felt better knowing that Donald was at the controls though I immediately buckled Madelyn's belt as tightly as possible, as I did my own, and I looked for a place for both of us to hold, knowing Donald as I did.

In a few minutes Captain Dunn pointed to a specific spot on the rolling waters as though he knew precisely where this LATITUDE ZERO lay. He nodded to Donald to "Pay his respects to Neptune."

Donald settled down a bit in his seat, straightened his shoulders, gave it the gun and away we went, straight up, both motors spitting fire. He leveled off and waited a minute for a last O.K. from Captain Dunn and Captain Dunn hesitated, not being quite sure that he was making the right decision. But then he nodded his consent. Away we went again, this time straight down. Then straight up. My baby screamed, "Daddy is going up over zero again to slide down the other side!" She squealed and held her stomach as her father dived and slipped the airliner towards the sea. She hid her head in her arms as we roared toward the water and she squealed again for fear the waves would splash in her face.

The Sikorsky dived at the waves then pulled up in a steep climb only to slide off in a slip. She side slipped to port. She side slipped to starboard. I feared lest Donald roll and loop and spin the Sikorsky as he had rolled and looped and spun his Jenny.

Again she shot straight up in the sky and again gravity mashed us into red leather as we roared into the Realms of Jupiter Rex. Hurricane rode the Sikorsky as she plummeted to within a razor's edge of the water, to within a feather of the Realms of Neptune, God of the Sea. Freedom! Wild reckless freedom!

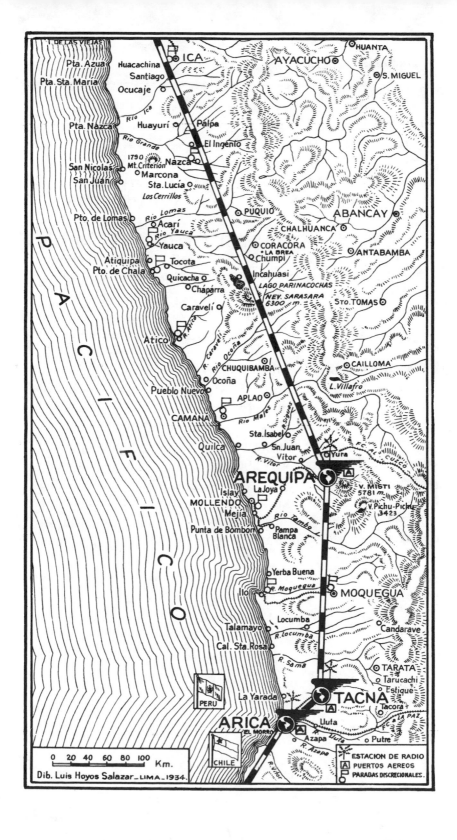

I. DE LAS VIEJAS

Pta. Azua
Pta. Sta. Maria

Huacachina
Santiago
Ocucaje

ICA

AYACUCHO

HUANTA

S. MIGUEL

Pta. Nazca

Rio Ica

Huayurí

Pálpa

El Ingento

San Nicolás
San Juan

1790
Mt. Criterion

Rio Grande

Nazca

Marcona
Sta. Lucía
Los Cerrillos

PUQUIO

ABANCAY

Pto. de Lomas

Rio Lomas

Acarí
Rio Yauca

Yauca

CHALHUANCA

CORACORA
LA BREA
Chumpi

ANTABAMBA

Atiquipa
Pto. de Chala

Tocota

Quicacha

Incahuasi

LAGO PARINACOCHAS

STO. TOMAS

Cháparra

N. EV. SARASARA
6300 m.

Caravelí

Atico

R. Atico

R. Caravelí

CAILLOMA

CHUQUIBAMBA

Ocoña

L. Villafro

R. Ocoña

Pueblo Nuevo

APLAO

Rio Majes

FC.A.CUZCO

CAMANA

Quilca

Sta. Isabel

Sn. Juan
Vitor

R. Vitor

Yura

Rio Camaná

AREQUIPA

V. MISTI
5781 m.

Islay
MOLLENDO
Mejía

La Joya

V. Pichu-Pichu
3423

Punta de Bombom

Rio Tambo

Pampa
Blanca

Yerba Buena

Ilo

R. Moquegua

MOQUEGUA

Locumba

Talamayo

Candarave

Cal. Sta. Rosa

R. Locumba

R. Sama

TARATA
Tarucachi
Estique

La Yarada

TACNA

Tacora

ARICA
EL MORRO

Lluta

LA PAZ

R. Lluta

Azapa

Putre

R. Azapa

PERU

R. Vítor

CHILE

0   20 40 60 80 100   Km.

Dib. Luis Hoyos Salazar_LIMA_1934.

ESTACION DE RADIO
PUERTOS AEREOS
PARADAS DISCRECIONALES.

P A C I F I C O

We Roman-candled our way back into the clouds. For a moment we floated aloft, quietly preening, readying for formal presentation to the Court of Neptune. Then we swan dived to the Point of Latitude Zero. A ROYAL SALUTE FROM THE EMPYREAN REALMS OF JUPITER REX, KING OF THE HEAVENS, RULER OF THE WINDS, MASTER OF ALL THINGS ABOVE THE EARTH. A ROYAL SALUTE TO HIS EXALTED MAJESTY, MIGHTY GOD OF THE SEA, NEPTUNE.

The next instant LATITUDE ZERO was behind us, north of us and we were on our way UP SOUTH. Captain Dunn said he always thought the Sikorsky would perform as it had done. He was delighted to know that it would though he himself never would try it. He said that he truly enjoyed the salute to Neptune. Probably Neptune never had such a salute, and most probably Neptune never again would have such a salute. However, if anything came of it, he would blame Donald.

I too was glad to know that the Sikorsky would not come apart. For that was good to know. Now we knew it. In years to come, when Donald was to test-fly Sikorskys and make delivery flights with them to Panagra, I didn't worry a bit. For I had seen a Sikorsky airliner put through the paces of spectacular and graceful acrobatics, and it did not come apart.

The third day came, the third day's flying from Panama to Chile, and we bade farewell to our now close friend, Steve. He said to Madelyn, "Goodbye, kid. Keep your Papa off the Equator!"

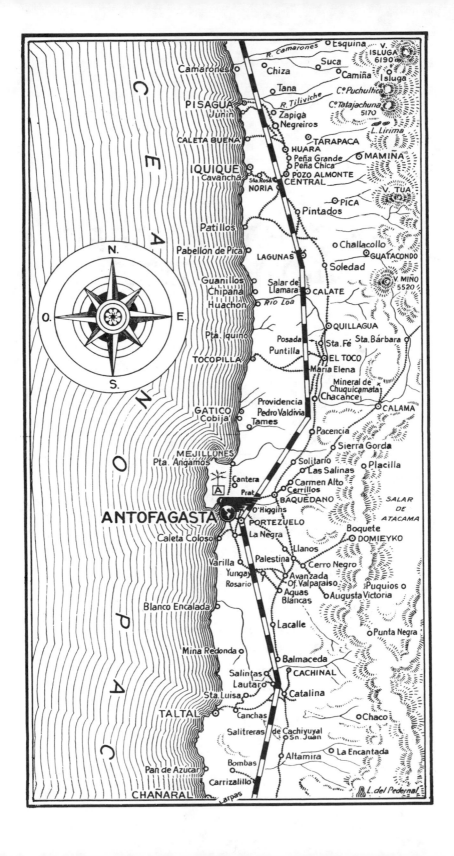

THE GREAT ANDEAN PILOT, SMITTY

Our third day south! Another day of newness to me. First in this newness was the giant trimotored Ford that awaited us in Talara, port of entry to Peru. I never had seen any aircraft as large as this, and at first sight it was awesome. It stood like a locomotive in a freight yard, its three motors ticking rhythmically in synchronization. What pilot could fly such a monster? What man would have the strength to pull it off the ground? "Mommie, it's big," Madelyn said, and she held tightly to my hand.

We had been told that our pilot would be Captain Warren Smith, chief pilot of the Southern Division of Panagra. As I stood and looked at the Ford I hoped that he would be a big and strong man, for what other kind could handle this trimotored giant?

Captain Smith arrived and he was more than big and strong. He was tremendous. A young man in his mid-twenties, he was precisely what I wanted for my pilot.

He came to us with a grin, he shook Donald's hand with both of his, welcoming him to his division of Panagra, and he spoke warmly to me. I addressed him, of course, as "Captain Smith." "Call me Smitty," he replied. "Everybody does."

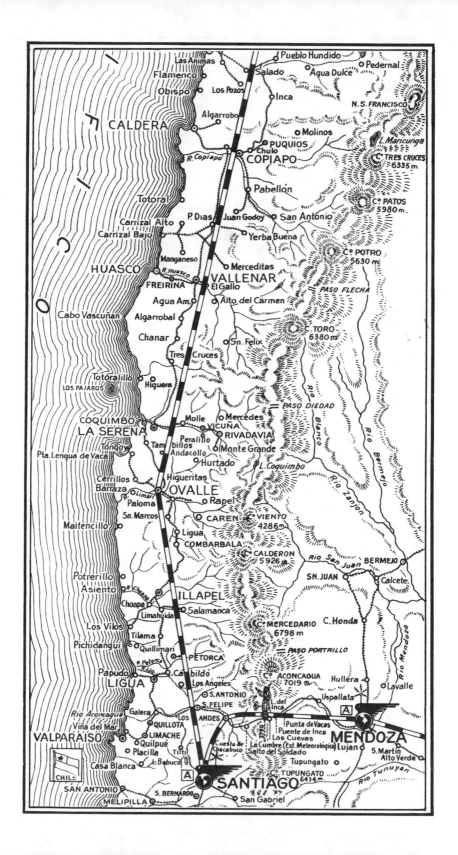

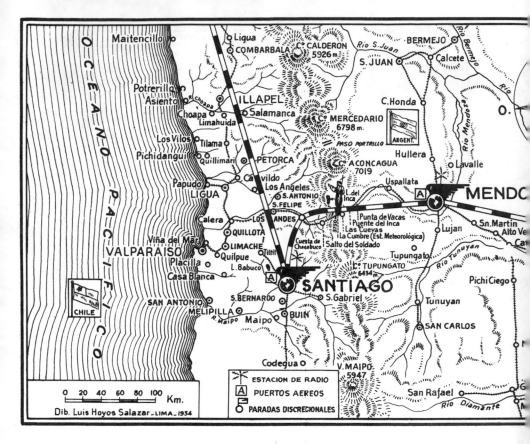

ESTACION DE RADIO
PUERTOS AEREOS
PARADAS DISCRECIONALES

Dib. Luis Hoyos Salazar_LIMA_1934

He picked Madelyn up in his big arms, asking her if she wanted to see inside the cockpit where her daddy would sit. He did not wait for an answer. "Come on, baby doll, let's go see the clocks in your daddy's cockpit. You like clocks, heh?"

She said, excitedly, "Smitty, my daddy climbed way up over Zero," she reached her arms up to show how high, "and he slid down the other side!"

"Yeah, I heard about that. Honey, let's not tell that."

"Smitty, will you climb up over Zero and slide down the other side?"

"Shhhhhhhhhhh! Let's go look at the clocks, huh?"

She put her arms around his neck, squeezed, and said, close in his face, "I want to slide. I want to slide some more!"

154

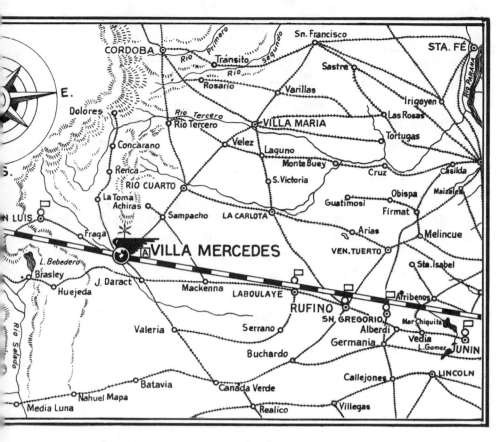

"Baby doll, don't you try to sweet talk me."

"I want to slide," she pouted quietly. I hoped she would not kick and scream, but she knew that Smitty would not, no matter how loudly she screamed. She settled for the clocks and hugged him again. It was clear to see that she adored this strong young man, Smitty.*

---

*Dear Reader,

Smitty had a little girl just Madelyn's size, but his little girl, Nannette, could not walk, for she had had polio. And his little girl was adopted. Smitty had adopted a little lame orphan girl. "But someday she will walk, just you wait and see."

Many years later we visited Nannette, who lived in Florida. She was married to a successful engineer, had two handsome sons, and walked with only a slight limp. It was as Smitty had said, "Someday Nannette will walk."

It was a happy-sad visit, for so many of Smitty's things were around the house. Only things—and memories. For death had claimed this greatest of all Andean pilots, Captain Warren B. Smith.

It was a happy takeoff. I felt so secure with Smitty in the left side of the cockpit. He sat quietly for a few minutes as the motors warmed. He took his time observing instruments, checking the controls, settling himself comfortably into his plush blue pilot's seat. Smitty seemed to be an installed section of the Ford, riveted in and unremovable. With an easy spread of one big hand he firmly grasped three throttles, using big thick fingers to hold each throttle separately controllable, and he brought the same three motors into perfect synchronization.

He turned and looked at us, with a wink and a nod that said, "Here we go! Hold on!"

His two big thumbs signaled "OUT" to the ground crew, and they pulled the chocks from the wheels. The Ford rolled its way down the field and with a sudden burst of power lazily lifted itself off the sod. Effortlessly, without haste, it began to climb. On to Lima, the midpoint between Cristobal, Panama, and Santiago, Chile.

Donald was to remain in Lima until he received his instrument flying test from Captain Thomas Jardine, chief pilot of the Central Division of Panagra. It was a gruelling test, lasting for hours each day for several consecutive days. The test was given in a tandem-cockpit, single-engine Fairchild. Captain Jardine occupied the front cockpit and gave his instructions by means of a gosport speaking tube. The pilot being tested flew "blind"; for the back cockpit, where he sat, was totally enclosed, with all its interior painted black to completely cut out visibility. The constant blind maneuvering, with blind takeoffs and blind landings, was not only a test of a pilot's ability but also of his stamina. There was no place in Panagra for fair weather pilots.

We checked in at the Hotel Bolivar until Donald completed his flight tests. Bolivar! Simon Bolivar! What memories. Simon, gone forever. No, not really gone, not

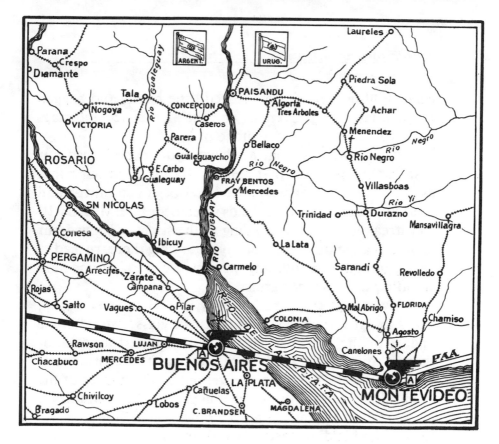

for me.

The hotel was of Spanish architecture, large and modern. It was ornate, with plush red draperies and heavy carved furniture. Our room was truly dramatic, with twelve foot ceilings and a huge four poster bed with a trundle bed for Madelyn. But it was cold and clammy, for the hotel had no heat. The bath was beautiful in ornate blue tile. It too was very large and had a seven-foot-long tub, the longest tub I had ever seen. And there was a bidet, my first experience with one. But the bathroom also was cold and clammy and there was no hot water. And there were no towels and no soap, for it was the custom for travelers to bring their own.

We went to the street and bought towels and soap, and we bought woolen ponchos to wear because it was so miserably cold. The streets were filled with beggars. Small lame children held out emaciated little hands and begged for pennies. It was overcast and the air was icy and stagnant, for the sun seldom shone in Lima.

It was in Lima that Madelyn and I experienced our first earthquake, our first temblor. We were in our room at the Hotel Bolivar when the hotel began to quiver and windows began to rattle. Maids screamed, "TEMBLOR!" and streaked from the building to the street. I opened our door and a maid, seeing Madelyn standing there, rushed in and grabbed her, pinning her to the door frame and shielding her with her arms.

I watched the curtains sway, the chandelier swing, heard things falling, heard the crash of glass. I stood in the middle of the room, so engrossed in the performance of the earthquake that I did not at first hear Madelyn screaming, "Mother! The nurse says get out of the middle of the room! Stand here with us under la puerta!" For Madelyn, it was instant Spanish. I moved quickly and stood, as did the maid, shielding Madelyn with my arms.

I heard a strange rumbling noise. It sounded like the beating of kettledrums and the roll of snares encased in an underground vault. It started in a muffled rumble and then swelled, as if orchestrated for a grand finale. Kettledrums rolled and a cymbal clashed as a heavy picture fell from the wall.

I thought that we should dash for the street, as I had seen others doing, and I motioned wildly to the maid in an effort to be understood. She was shaking her head and saying something in Spanish.

"Madelyn, what is she saying? Do you understand her?"

"She says it's too late! Stay under la puerta!"

The hotel shook violently. The huge ropero and other furniture shifted on the floor. Then the strange rumbling began gradually to fade away. The chandelier swung slowly,

158

curtains began to hang correctly, though not in place as they had been. The movement began to slow to a stop and finally all was quiet and still. Maids were returning to the hotel saying, "Por Dios! Por Dios!" Oh how I would hate to live in Lima! Indeed I never never would.

I did not mention the earthquake to Donald when he came in, for I hoped that Madelyn would attach no importance to it. But when we were in bed, Donald and I in the huge four-poster and Madelyn in the trundle bed by my side, she said, "Daddy, I'm scared. I want to sleep with you."

"Ah, baby!"

"Donald, she'll scream."

She did not wait for consent but climbed over me, squeezed in between us, and lay quiet, as though she were asleep. Then she sat up in bed and said, excitedly, "Daddy, this hotel had temblors. Does your airplane have temblors?" He said sometimes it felt as though it did.

"The mean old nurse wouldn't let me watch. The mean old nurse held me under la puerta and covered me up, so I couldn't watch!"

"Baby, go to sleep!"

"I don't want to go to sleep! I want to watch this hotel have a temblor!"

He said the hotel wouldn't have a temblor tonight, but she said, "Uh huh, yes it will!"

"Donald, now I'm scared. Do you think we'll have another earthquake?"

"The hotel will not have a temblor tonight," he repeated.

But Madelyn said, "Uh huh! Yes it will!"

And it did.

Donald was checked out as Airline Captain and we waited for the next flight south. When the Ford arrived, who would our Captain be but Smitty! We had not hoped for such luck, for he took only the flights across the High Andes from Santiago to Buenos Aires. But he had come to fly us home. Joyfully we continued "up south" to Santiago with Smitty, who was to become our lifelong friend.

Our first landing was at Arequipa, Peru, where we refueled and stretched our legs and arms. In the Ford one could stretch out almost straight, if one was as small as I. But there were taller passengers aboard who were more than delighted to walk a bit and swing their arms.

Our second landing was at Arica, the first port of entry into Chile. The landing at Arica was truly divine in its smoothness. How on earth could a pilot bring in such a giant of a Ford and land it as if it were down of a thistle! I searched for words to express my admiration to this huge young man, Smitty.

He said, "Yeah, that was all right, wasn't it?" And he winked at Madelyn as only Smitty could wink. Then with a roar of laughter, he said, "Tell her, baby doll, tell her your daddy made that landing. Tell her your daddy flew you into Chile."

It couldn't be! Not Donald, who always side-slipped to a landing. I said, "Donald, really, you weren't flying, were you?" He grinned as though he had done something he shouldn't, then said he sure as hell was, adding that he was checked out. "I'll have you know I am an airline pilot, and a damned good one!"

Donald flew as pilot, carrying us on to Santiago. It was truly an airline flight, with hardly a ripple to mar, or to liven up, the day. Smooth—smooth—airline smooth, almost boring perfection. "I want to slide!" Madelyn peevishly pouted.

At last, the end of a long quiet day, Santiago, our destination, Santiago, Chile, our home.

Personnel from the station came out to welcome us as

we landed, for they were expecting Captain Beatty. They were pleased to meet him, they said, and they were pleased to meet *La Senora* Beatty and *La Senorita* Madelyn. The traffic department asked for our baggage, and immigration inspectors were puzzled that we had so little luggage. "Was there some mistake, Captain Beatty?" No, there was no mistake for we had brought but one suitcase each, as Mr. MacGregor had requested.

Smitty picked up Madelyn in his big strong arms and tossed her into the air, laughing his great roaring laugh, "Baby doll, you are in God's country! Now you are La Senorita Madelyn!" She giggled with delight for she loved her new name and repeated it over and over. "I am La La Senorita Madelyn! I am La La La Senorita. Mommie, I am a song!"

I stood alone and looked around the field at Los Cerrillos. It was a cold, windy, barren spot, filled with smooth, round, black rocks brought down by the glacier, and it was completely encircled by a wall of giant Andean peaks that formed an impenetrable ice-hard fortress around it. I stood, so small, in so large a someplace that always had been and always would be, a land of forever.

The sun was setting behind this impenetrable fortress, leaving me within it. My life and all that I had known before was in a slow, darkening fadeout. I felt entrapped and imprisoned in this forever land and I was afraid.

Then, with a sudden burst of rainbow sunset, ice-lace curtains were sparkling and rising on my new world. Was I free? In God's Country? Was I La-La-La-Senora?

Dear Reader: In 1966 Nanette sent me this clipping:

The South Dade News Leader

WANT ADS—248-2511
247-2321 (Homestead)—235-8531 (Perrine) HOMESTEAD, FLA., TUESDAY, DECEMBER 6, 1966   Daily Home Delivery

Pilot's Ashes To Be Scattered Over Andes Mountains Of Chile

A last farewell to a pioneer of aviation, Redlands resident Capt. Warren B. Smith, will be given Dec. 12 as his ashes are scattered over the Andes Mountains of Chile over the route he flew for years.

Captain Smith, decorated twice by the Chilean government for services to that country, died in Miami of emphysema May 21, 1965, at age 62. Even after death he gave of himself: to the University of Miami Medical School for study of emphysema, and to the Lions Eye Bank for someone in need.

By his own wish, his ashes will be scattered over his beloved Andes on Chilean Air Force Day. They will be transported from Miami to Santiago by Panagra Airlines, for which he flew for many years, and then flown to El Cristo by the Chilean Air Force to be scattered over the mountains.

The captain's daughter, Mrs. R. A. (Nanette) Wulf of Tennessee Road in the Redlands, will accompany the ashes to Chile.

Capt. Smith had resided at 22700 Tennessee Road, where he owned an avocado grove, from 1947 until his death.

A native of Minnesota, he learned to fly in San Francisco in 1921 in military aviation. Later he flew around the country barn storming, then joined Gates Flying Circus.

He joined Panagra in 1931 and resided in Chile 6½ years. During those years he logged more than 2,000 crossings of the Andes, flying more than 30,000 people. The 20,597 hours he flew represents almost two and a half years in the air, and the miles flown, an astronomical figure of over 2 million.

VETERAN AVIATOR Warren B. Smith is shown at controls of plane, as he looked in years when he logged 2,000 crossings of Andes in Chile. Ashes of late Redlands resident will be scattered over Andes Mountains on Chilean Air Force Day, Dec. 12.

He was decorated by the Chilean government for his efforts in aiding the injured and maimed by removing over a thousand victims, mostly children. after the devastating Chilean earthquake of 1939.

He was decorated again after completing 1,000 crossings of the Andes between Santiago and Buenos Aires, Argentina, and given the title of "Caballero de los Andes." In recognition of his service to Chile, as avenue in Santiago was named after him, Avenida Warren Smith.

He retired as a pilot in the early 1950's, but remained with Panagra until early 1965, a few months before his death.

The Magnificent Christ of the Andes—A cristus, cast out of a metal cannon used in the last war between these neighbor nations, guards the Chilean-Argentine border. Its inscription reads, "Sooner shall these mountains crumble into dust than Argentines and Chileans break the peace. Sworn at the feet of Christ the redeemer."

GOD'S COUNTRY SANTIAGO, CHILE: OUR HOME

I found a most divine house for us in suburb Los Leones. Our home in Chile! Our beautiful casa, so lovely in its pink stucco Spanish architecture, with gardens and patios, all securely locked in by a high stone wall with ornate wrought-iron gates.

Our casa was large with many rooms. And there was a long wing for the servants' quarters, for all the servants lived there and seldom left, not even for a half day. Our beautiful Chilean casa of many rooms! But the room I loved best, the most handsome one, was our bedroom.

Chileans put great stock in the Master's bedroom, for in Chile it was the custom for Senor and his Senora to go to bed. And there was no furniture in Chile to equal the dramatic beauty of the "bed for the Master."

The bed for the Master was huge, conducive, with heavy carvings and with heavy red velvet cortinas. The bed for the Master had the masculine feel, the feel of no fluff. La Senora was in his bed, he was not in hers. The headboard was tufted, for Senora's comfort. The ceiling above the Master's bed was interestingly fanciful. La Senora could count the prisms on the chandelier, should she choose.—HO HUM!

Donald in Curtiss Falcon at Los Cerrillos, Santiago, Chile.

Our bedroom opened out onto a balcony facing east and it was there, on my balcony, that I dreamed my dreams and fought my fears.

Donald began his search flights immediately and I went with him to Los Cerrillos to watch his first take-off in the Fairchild, which was the plane used for search.

The Fairchild was a single-motored high-altitude plane, dubbed "Razor Back" for the shape of the fuselage. Truly it looked like an old Razor Back hog, and seemed just that mean. It had fold-back wings as though it meant to squeeze under the fence and escape into the pasture. Old Razor Back!

But don't let names mislead you. I saw it take off, like a bullet, in a short space of runway. I watched it climb like a World War fighter plane, straight for combat with the peaks of the High Andes. It ballooned like a kite in a wind stream and its powerful Wasp engine, with low pitch props, sent it on its way, up, up, up, up where the oxygen breathing tubes felt good between the teeth. I did not feel left behind; with a choice I would not have chosen this wild adventure.

Old Razor Back, with wings folded, sets in Panagra hangar, Santiago, Chile.

167

THE SEARCH FOR THE SAN JOSE...
from the notes of Capt. Donald Beatty

*Donald C. Beatty
in high-altitude
Curtiss "Falcon."*

When claims are made that flights over the Andes and particularly "flying the hump," as the high-point of the Uspallata Pass is called, are the "toughest flights in aviation," one visualizes the fog-covered Alleghenies, the blizzard-swept passes of the Sierra Nevadas, the Rockies, and the Cascade mountains. Uspallata Pass, with its highest point at the Cumbre near the famous Christ of the Andes statue is the granddaddy of them all! Like a funnel at both ends, the Pass narrows in places to a jagged granite-walled gorge less than three hundred feet wide! It has everything known in the weather line—ice, snowstorms lasting for weeks, thin air, cold air, fog, rain, and clouds, plus a terrific turbulence. On occasion a forceful thought, sometimes brought to mind during a crossing, could likely be "now let us pray...!" While Uspallata Pass provides a shorter route between Chile's capital city Santiago and the great wine center and a port of entry into Argentina at Mendoza, it is considerably higher and a great deal more rugged than the other somewhat easier pass, Paso de Maipú, some one hundred miles to the south. The latter was completely devoid of habitation even in its lowest approaches and consequently Uspallata was used at all times except when emergency conditions prevailed.

Panagra management had originally planned for the search plane to be crewed by but one person—an experienced "instrument" pilot familiar with flying in un-mapped areas but who also was expert in radio telegraphy. I fulfilled the requirement. The search plane?—a model 71 Fairchild monoplane known as a "razor back" because of its peculiarly shaped fuselage—triangular, with the apex at the top. Arranged similarly to a Navy carrier-type aircraft, its wings folded back over the pointed or sharp top center edge of the fuselage. Power plant?—a single Pratt & Whitney Wasp engine arranged for high altitude flight. Equipped with a "tooth pick" or flat pitch propeller, the installation permitted high RPM with an instant application of power, an absolute essential for low-level flight among the rugged peaks and glaciers of the high Andes. Instruments for "blind flying"?—turn and bank, rate of

The cold gold of morning.

climb, and an air speed indicator, the basic minimum requirement. A sensitive altimeter and compass were also installed—period! Communications?—a radio telegraph key would be attached to a leg clamp which would fit just above the knee of the pilot!

It took but one flight over the proposed search area to convince me that the plan to use a single crew member for the search plane just simply would not work. I found that the ever-present clear air turbulence during low level flight in the mountains was terrific and could be compared, in a manner of speaking, with the multitudinous jerks and jolts one would experience in "breaking" a wild Brahma bull penned inside a falling elevator jolting to a sudden stop at the bottom of its shaft because of a broken supporting cable. I found I needed one of my hands on the "stick," one on the throttle (the engine would "over-rev" from sudden tail-wind

170

Sunrise High Style.

Swing Low Sweet Chariot, through the Uspallata Pass.

Storms "head him off at the pass."

type turbulence), one to hang on with, and one to make the "sign of the cross" while negotiating, at low level, most of the canyons, glaciers, and peaks of those TALL hills!

Instrument flight was essential even in perfectly clear air! Looking down into treeless canyons of the mountains, the eye is inclined to make the slope of the hills in the horizon line. Lakes in the bottom of some of the canyons appear to be definitely "slanting" whether they are ice-covered or not. The down drafts often accompanying clear air turbulence frequently cause the mountainside to seem to rise up before you. There was no sudden jar, but a sensation as in a rapidly descending elevator. Sometimes in less than twenty or twenty-five seconds the altimeter would show that the aircraft had dropped 4,000 to 5,000 feet in that time. . . . again, even with throttle closed, a similar turbulence would cause the aircraft to gain that much altitude in a like period of time.

Sunrise spots the blue crystal glacier.

The glacier spreads in iridescence.

Andean storms move in to black out Aconcagua.

Since the objective of the search flights was to locate a downed aircraft and not to engender a second, two additional experts were added to the search crew—a flight radio operator and a professional photographer/observer. Thousands of photographs of areas which appeared likely to hold remnants of the lost *San Jose* were subseqently made during the many months of the search. These were projected onto a large theater-type screen back at the Santiago headquarters and scrutinized thoroughly for any sign of the wreckage.

Why the search flights? The missing *San Jose*, a tri-motored Ford airliner with 15 persons aboard, had flown into oblivion during a regularly scheduled transandean flight. It had taken off from Santiago

174

The eternal white realms of Jupiter Rex.

without incident. Destination was Montevideo,
Uruguay with an intermediate stop at Buenos Aires.
The route for the capitol of Chile to the Argentina
port of entry at Mendoza was via the famed Uspallata
Pass through the highest ranges of the Andes mountains. A few miles to the south of the pass is Cerro
Tupungato which rises in a jagged snow-clad cone
almost 23,000 feet above the sea. Rough ranges of
over 20,000 feet connect Tupungato with the famed
monach of the Andes— Mount Aconcagua, spot-
lessly white, sharply cut against an azure sky and
towering almost 24,000 feet above the sea. A somewhat narrow "V" in the ranges between the two
giant peaks is "la Cumbre," the summit or high
point of the Pass. Width of the bottom of the "V" is
approximately 250 feet—both sides rise steeply to
the crest of the jagged ranges at the 20,000-foot plus
level. The gorge on the Chilean side of the Cumbre
is almost vertical—terrain drops down abruptly for
several thousand feet from the Cumbre while it is

175

The search crew for the San Jose.

somewhat less on the Argentine side.

In addition to passengers and crew, the *San Jose* carried several hundred pounds of valuable platinum "pigs" addressed to a bank group in Europe, and mail and express for Argentina, Uruguay and Brazil. The veteran pilot of the ill-fated flight was Captain Robinson, who had great experience in the transandean operations and was in fact manager of that division. He was a thoroughly seasoned airman and had frequently captained similar transandean flights.

Top priority was given to locating the lost airliner, its victims, and valuable cargo. Argentine law required that persons missing as result of a catastrophe could not be declared legally dead nor

The High Andes—a rhapsody in ice.

Which ones in all the world have been higher than the mountaintop?

Peaks of the Andes rose 23,000 feet in the sky, higher than any plane could fly.

could their estates be settled until after a period of twenty years from the date of such a tragedy. Bank accounts and other assets of those aboard the missing *San Jose* were thus frozen by law, which placed great hardship upon some of the families of those missing. Salaries of flight crews were continuing and the company provided funds to financially distressed families of those listed on the passenger manifest. Locating the lost plane and establishing the status of those aboard was thus a paramount objective.

End Notes—D.C.B.

It was a happy time—Donald in his element with Old Razor Back in the Wild Blue Yonder; I in mine, my calm pink casa with my pink beribboned little Madelyn.

I turned my attention solely to my casa for there were servants to be selected, furniture to be bought, clothes to be made.

First to sewing women, for neither Madelyn nor I had clothes, having come with only a suitcase in hand. Three sewing women came at once and within a short time Madelyn and I had beautiful clothes, though different from those we had in Alabama. Madelyn had dozens of brightly embroidered dresses with matching pinafores and I was most elegant in my French silks and satins and laces and a black velvet with train—my dresses were cut very very low in the neck, scandalously low, much lower than any I had ever worn before. But this was the custom in Chile. Donald liked it.

Jose came to us as butler. At that time, he was in the service of bachelor John Shannon, manager of the Southern Division of Panagra. John enthusiastically recommended Jose for his honesty, integrity, proficiency, and training. Jose was the perfect butler for us. Bachelor Shannon would find himself another man servant.

If Jose was such a jewel, why would John be so eager to let him go? John admitted, bluntly, that Jose was profoundly Puritan and therefore a lousy butler for a bachelor, such as himself. He had been wondering for some time how to get rid of Jose and this was the perfect solution. If Donald would employ Jose, John would be eternally grateful.

Bachelor Shannon was a notch higher than Donald on the organization chart of Panagra. Donald hired Jose without argument.

Mrs. Burgan came to us as Madelyn's governess. Mrs. Burgan was herself Chilean but her husband was

English. He was the British consul at Tumaco, Chile. She preferred to be called Mrs. Burgan and not Senora Burgan. Why she came to us as governess I did not know. She was beautifully educated and she was a very handsome Senora. She taught Madelyn dancing, music, Spanish, French, and German. She slept in an adjoining room to Madelyn's and she had her meals in the children's dining room. This gave her the top social position among the servants.

My main problem at this time was adjusting to having so many servants, sewing women, maids, cooks, and gardeners besides Mrs. Burgan and Jose. I did not want so many servants, "empleados." All of them were white. Of course none of them spoke English, and my Spanish was very inadequate. What little vocabulary I knew was social Spanish and had little to do with daily routine household affairs.

I also had to adjust to having little or no authority with the empleados for it was the Chilean custom for the man of the house to control the empleados and the running of the casa. But Donald had his hands full of Fairchild and down drafts, and he was not about to take on the chores of housekeeping. Housekeeping was my department. The casa and the empleados were strictly my concern, not his.

But the empleados would take no directives from me. They sat, and did nothing, until Donald came. The first day he was out of Santiago no food was brought, no cleaning was done, no clothes were washed. In twenty-four hours our casa was in utter confusion and chaos, for no empleado dared move without orders from Capitan Beatty.

I tried to explain to them, in my ever growing Spanish vocabulary, that I, La Senora, would direct the housekeeping. But they only exploded in their own Chilean way and wrung their hands.

I phoned the Panagra Office and told the office manager my predicament. He understood, for this always happened with Americans in Chile. He himself came, immediately, and calling all my empleados together, explained to them that they were not to wait for Capitan Beatty. They were to take orders from La Senora, for that was the custom in Estados Unidos.

This did not set well with them, for it was to lose face to take orders from a woman. So, since Jose understood my Spanish, I turned the running of the house over to him. And he ran my casa as he would a country club, no party being too large for him to handle and no party materializing too suddenly for him to manage.

Jose did indeed run my casa as though it were a country club. And at times it seemed to be exactly that.

It was becoming more and more fashionable for the "elite" from the States to fly this new airline, Panagra, for Panagra not only flew over seas and High Andes, it also flew across the Equator, which no other airline had ever done. Celebrities were coming into Santiago, often with Mr. MacGregor or some other official from the Panagra office in New York, or even from Grace Line, or Pan American Airways. And it became the custom for them to call, from Los Cerillos, to say they just had landed, and to ask if eight or ten Panagra passengers might invite themselves to have dinner with us that night.

They were always enthusiastically welcomed and Jose took great pride in preparing eight-course dinners for these spontaneous occasions. Often he would have a fire built in the center of the garden and he would throw woolen fringed saddle blankets on the grass, where guests could sit by the fire, after dinner, and drink Chilean Underrauga wine and sing.

News got around that, when in Santiago, the thing to do, if you could wangle an invitation, was to go to Captain

Beatty's for dinner. Captain Beatty's "Pilot's Luck" guest book soon filled with names to remember. Pilots' wives swooned with the thought of having Clark Gable for a dinner partner. And one enthusiastic guest, Will Rogers, visaed Donald's passport, saying it was "good when sober." This gave trouble at times, for there were immigration officials who had never heard of Will Rogers.

Jose loved flowers and our home was full of them at all times. One night, when (unexpectedly) Baron Rothschild and friends were coming to dinner, Jose was most disturbed that our flowers were a bit wilted. However, when our guests arrived, the house was ablaze with fresh flowers. The next morning, when I commended Jose for the fine banquet he had given us, I spoke particularly of his handsome flower arrangements.

"I don't know how you managed, on such short notice," I said.

"Ah, Senora," he replied proudly, "I climbed the wall and stole them from the gardens of the French Embassy."

"Jose! You must not steal their flowers!"

"Senora, it was so dark. No one saw me."

It was the custom in Chile for the butler to be ever present in the living room, as well as in the dining room. And it was expected of the butler to anticipate the "Patron's" every need. At first I found it very awkward and difficult having Jose standing in the living room with Donald and me, at all times the perfect chaperone. But since Jose spoke no English, Donald and I talked freely in his presence. This too was difficult for me to accept, for Donald and I had many personal comments to make, and it seemed strange having a rather young, almost handsome man listening, at all times. Sometimes I wondered if Jose did understand English and if he was not enjoying what he heard.

There were times when I wished he would go away. But to go away was not the custom in Chile. He would stand his grounds and remain with us, whether or not we liked it. I even found it difficult to practice on my Steinway, for Jose stood adamantly in the corner of the room, as a silent reminder that I should need something, maybe a sweater or maybe a Martini. The only place Donald and I could go to get away from Jose was in our bed. I never decided if this was good or bad.

THE SEARCH FOR
THE *SAN JOSE*

From the beginning Donald loved the search flights, the high altitude flying. He loved everything about the High Andes, the violence of it all. He was completely confident that he would find the *San Jose*. Somewhere he would spot a piece of it, some remnant of it, or some clue as to where it lay buried in the snow and ice. For it was there, somewhere up in those frozen lands above the sky, in some crevasse, under some precipice, in some ravine. He would find it, for all it took was a bit of daring.

He flew low over high snow peaks and into deep frozen crevasses, and he combed the glacier, flying low enough to see well. He flew low enough to create avalanches with his prop wash, for he would clear away the snow in order to uncover the *San Jose*. Though buried in the snow it lay, he would find it. He was so confident. Each morning, just before dawn, when the Panagra bus came for him, Donald was impatiently waiting to begin another search flight. Finding the *San Jose* was becoming a compulsion.

When we were in our pillows, and away from Jose, he said to me, "Sweetheart, I flew directly over our casa this morning. Did you hear me?"

184

"Of course I heard you, and I saw you. Didn't you see me waving to you from my balcony?"

"I didn't look to see. I thought you had gone back to sleep. I wanted to wake you up."

"You know I never go back to sleep after you leave. I can't sleep when you are flying the Andes. When I heard Old Razor Back, I ran to my balcony and waved to you. Why didn't you buzz my balcony?"

"I will buzz your balcony tomorrow morning, I will for sure."

"If you do, would you lose your job?"

He said he sure as hell would, and that he wouldn't buzz my balcony because he liked his job.

Each morning, just before day's first light, Donald flew over our casa. The Fairchild swooped a low dip to me, and every morning I waved to it. And with a slight shudder of fear, I watched from my balcony as the single-motored Fairchild flew into the sunrise and disappeared over the High Andes.

At first Donald flew the search flights alone, being pilot, radio operator, navigator, and observer, all in one. But after several weeks of flying into the unbelievable turbulence of the High Andes, his flying alone was discontinued, and a crew was assigned to him.

I was amazed at the stories he told me at night when we were together alone in our bed, away from Jose. He told me of the updrafts, the down drafts, with winds that pitched Old Razor Back as a foaming surf pitches a beach ball. He needed one hand on the bottom of the seat to keep from being slung into the hereafter. I wished I could go with him! Then again I was glad I could not, for this sort of flying was over my head and I wasn't sure I even liked hearing about it.

After weeks and weeks of this Donald was beginning to come home, night after night, in a state of exhaustion I never had seen in him before. I was sorry he had taught me to fly so long ago, in 1923. I was sorry I knew what a Jenny, with an OX5 motor, would have done in the High Andes. I was sorry I knew what torture a single-motored Fairchild could endure. I was beginning to feel fear of his flying all day, every day in the single-motored Fairchild, searching for the *San Jose*, searching for the pattern of the storm that had destroyed it.

The snows were estimated to be more than 500 feet deep, and the temperature was estimated to be more than 100 degrees below zero. How could Donald, day after day, deliberately fly into the perpetual hurricanes of the High Andes, just to chart their courses? How could he seek out updrafts that would fling him like a stone from a slingshot into the sky beyond? How could he seek to locate down drafts and skim the edges of them when those down drafts could so easily lick out and suck him into their undertow? I knew that if that one Wasp engine faltered, or failed, Donald would disappear, just as Captain Robinson and the *San Jose* had disappeared. How could he take such chances with his life—and with mine!

But the *San Jose* would be found, and he would find it. After each flight he meticulously analyzed his findings. He carefully charted the wind currents he had encountered, and concluded there was a slight chance that the *San Jose* had been catapulted, completely off course, into a different area of the Andes, for anything was possible in the cyclonic winds of an Andean storm.

He increased the circle of the search. He mapped and charted vast areas of the Andes that no man had ever seen before, vast areas that were marked on the maps of South America simply as UNKNOWN. Old Razor Back was the first to roar into this unknown sanctuary of Jupiter Rex. And Donald's eyes were the first to see this vast, glorious frigid Sky Primeval. I prayed that Jupiter Rex would not, in his wrath, dash him back to earth where man belonged.

One night when we were in our pillows, away from Jose, I said to him that he was pushing it too hard in his determination to find the *San Jose*. I thought it was better that it be left alone, buried in the snow and ice, where it was. Who could doubt that there were no survivors?

I said, "Honey, you are flying too many hours a day, and every day, with too little oxygen, or with no oxygen at all. How can you hope to win always? One miscalculation—that is all it takes—just one miscalculation. I worry so much."

He said I should stop worrying, that he could handle anything the Andes could hand out to him. He said that I would feel differently about it if he could take me up with him, just once. If I could feel the winds pitch the Fairchild into an updraft and feel the Fairchild hit the serviceable ceiling, then beyond, into the absolute ceiling—and still

The turbulent Uspallata Pass—140 miles long, 250 feet wide.

If that one engine falters or fails...

beyond, where power controls cease to function. Then feel the sinking back, where the controls of power catch again. "Today," he said, "I was flung into rolls like no roll I ever encountered before. Three times my trailing antenna was wrapped around the fuselage. I landed with it still wrapped around."

I did not remember ever flying with a trailing antenna, for I never remember ever having a radio.

"All that sounds great," I said, "but all the same you are pushing too hard. One of these days I am going to say, NO! you can't fly so much. You are so sure you can handle anything the Andes can deal out to you. Suppose I said NO! Could you handle that?"

He said he could handle me, that I was a pushover. I always had been a pushover.

"But you never have heard me say NO. How can you be so certain you can handle that?"

He said he was certain. "Try me. Say NO to me."

I tried him. I said, "Captain Beatty, NO!"

And I said again, "Captain Beatty, NO! NO!"

And I said again, "NO! NO! NO!" to a laughing man with deaf ears.

I had to find some place to get away from Jose, besides this bed!

DOWN DRAFTS

The Beautiful Senoritas, The Eager Senores

We were beginning to make Chilean friends and to be invited into the social circles of Santiago. Chileans were handsome people. The Senoritas were like alabaster dolls, with their delicate, cream-like skins and their long, straight, black hair, and their clothes made of costly French materials. The Senoras were ladened with diamonds and emeralds.

They were slender graceful women, and I wasn't so sure we American women were quite their equals in appearance. Standing close beside them did not compliment us, and I learned early to put some distance between them and me so that the contrast would be less visible.

I could not see at all why the Chilean men admired the American women so much, or why they were so attentive to us. But the wives of Panagra captains were strictly in demand at all social functions. We had a never-ending supply of dance partners for tangos or waltzes.

Once I asked Mrs. Burgan about it. "Why is it that the Chilean men dance with American women so much, and dance so much less with their own beautiful women?"

She was surprised that I should ask. "Ah, Senora, the American women do not wear corsets. Chilean men like that.''

"Then if Chilean men do not like corsets why in heaven's name do Chilean women wear them? Why would they strap themselves into harnesses, especially when they have such beautiful figures? Where on earth is the advantage?''

"But, Senora, that is the custom! No respectable Senora would ever go without a corset!''

All this time I had thought the Chilean men were dancing with me because I was such a good dancer.

"Mrs. Burgan, tell me, verdad, do I tango well or do Chilean men dance with me only because I don't wear a corset?''

"Ah, Senora, it is both! You tango so well and you—you—you—''

Mrs. Burgan would not put it into words. She wouldn't come right out and say that I "felt so good.''

I wasn't at all sure that I wanted to "feel so good.'' And I decided then and there that I would buy a corset and wear it always. I would be like a respectable Chilean Senora. And while I was at it I would order some crocheted brassieres like the ones the Senoras wore. These lace-like lovelies, crocheted in double and chain stitch, came in all colors. There was a large round hole in the center of each cup, so that the nipples would not be suppressed, but rather would protrude through the holes and give added interest to a low cut dress (pointed reminders).

That afternoon I went to Los Cerillos to meet Donald when he came in after the search, and I was wearing my corset. he squeezed me hello. "What on earth happened to you!'' he said. "I bought a corset. Look!'' I turned around proudly for him to see me completely strapped in. "Do you like it?'' He said he sure as hell did not like it.

I wondered again why the lovely Senoras would not go without a corset. Suddenly I knew. They, like most of my friends and me, were monogamous. They chose their men carefully and they did not want to "feel so good" to just any man who cared to dance. While I thought this was carrying monogamy a bit far, I would wear my corset always, when Donald was out of town, for I wanted to be a respectable Senora.

Mrs. Burgan told me many things that I should know, although she was reluctant to do so, I being La Senora of la casa. But one day she mustered up courage enough to tell me, that although I was La Senora, I should not refer to Captain Beatty as El Senor. "Why?" I asked. "If I am La Senora why is not Captain Beatty El Senor?" She hesitated a long time, in her embarrassment. Finally she said, "Senora, in Chile El Senor means Jesus Christ." Jeepers Creepers! for months I had called Donald Jesus Christ!

Every morning just before daybreak, the Panagra bus was at the door to take Captain Beatty to Los Cerillos. This daily search lasting for hours was a suicidal schedule, although it was Donald's choosing and no one's choosing but his own. Each morning when I watched from my balcony as he flew over our casa and disappeared over the Andes, I was more than wide awake. I was more than worried. I was more than afraid.

I would stand on my balcony with the icy wind in my face, fearing to take my eyes off the spot where I last saw the Fairchild, hoping it would return. Donald was logging approximately 140 hours a month in the High Andes. By any yardstick that was suicidal. Smitty put a stop to it by placing Donald on the regular scheduled run to Buenos Aires. This gave Donald rest days in Santiago as well as rest days in B.A. I was so grateful to Smitty! I was so happy!

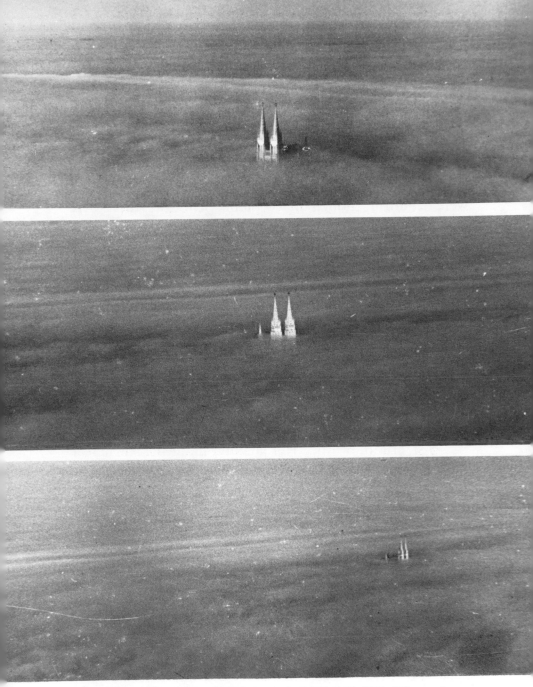

A WELCOME SIGHT FOR A LOST PILOT. The spire of the cathedral of Buenos Aires, a beacon reaching through the dark, flashing in the sun, proclaiming I AM THE WAY.

But bits of conversation here and there between Panagra pilots and sly jokes, with in-between meanings, made me suddenly aware of down drafts that never before had entered my mind. There were dangers in glamorous Buenos Aires, Argentina. There were night clubs and casinos filled with beautiful and willing Senoritas. There were beautiful, though unacceptable Senoritas, there were beautiful and most socially acceptable Senoritas who found handsome airline captains an irresistible prize. What young man would not turn a head in the direction of such hero worship? There were deadly down drafts in Buenos Aires, Argentina.

I asked Anabel what she thought of this. She said she didn't think about it very often, she just tried to stay out of trouble in Santiago. "We have a wide choice of eager Senores here who think nothing at all of stealing a pilot's wife." She named several whom I knew.

"Anabel! What woman would want those men! They are so crude!"

"Si, crudo, bruto." Her laughter made me feel naive. "Honey child, this is not Alabama."

She gave this time to soak in, then she asked, "Have you read *The Road to Buenos Aires*?"

I had not even heard of it. She went to the bookcase and brought out a cheap book. "Don't tell Donald I gave it to you." I thumbed through, read a few pages. It described the luxuries of the goverment operated houses of Argentina, so plushly decorated, with red brocades, with mirrored walls surrounding the beds. It described the charm of the "madams"—the frivolity of the girls—varying delights could be had for varying prices. I put the book back into the bookcase because it did not entertain me. "Anabel, this sort of thing is no threat to me. Tell me about the socially acceptable Senoritas in B.A. Lovely brunettes, no doubt."

"Si, Senora! And blonds also. Gentlemen prefer blonds, and blonds prefer airline captains. So do brunettes." She laughed as though she dared any of them to compete for Smitty. I would not dare them to compete with me for Donald, for the High Andes were on their side.

I was to learn that Anabel was most accurate in the findings, for Senoritas, both blond and brunette, did indeed prefer airline captains. And there were many eager Senores who thought nothing at all of stealing an airline captain's wife. One evening, at dinner, I said to Donald, who just had returned from several days in B.A. "Donald, did you know that Dick and Ruth are getting a divorce?"

"No. Why?"

"Dick has a Senorita bedded and boarded in B.A. Ruth heard about it and lashed back. Now Ruth has an eager Senor in Santiago. Dick swears he'll kill that Chilean S.O.B."

"Who told you that?"

"Anabel."

"You know that isn't true!"

"Yes it is, because Smitty grounded Dick, until Dick could get his love life straightened out. It's dangerous to fly with a pilot who has his mind set on killing his wife's lover."

"Who told you that?"

"Anabel. Donald, this is wild country. There are too many willing Senoritas in B.A. and too many eager Senores in Santiago. The bonds of holy matrimony are frail."

He voiced his opinion of Ruth, and I said that I thought Ruth was wise.

"So! You believe in Free Love!"

"Love isn't free, it's costly, bought only with true love in return." And I pointed out that play in bed wasn't free either, that a man could beget costly problems in bed, as Dick had found out.

This was a stupid subject. I wished I hadn't brought it up, and I tried to change it, but Donald had sunk his teeth in it and was lashing out at Ruth. I lashed back, "Tell me about the Senoritas in B.A. I worry about your being there, for any woman in her right mind would want a handsome airline pilot, even though he be my husband."

The subject was dropped. Jose poured wine and busied himself with plates and things. Donald did not like what he was hearing, but Jose did, and it was then that I knew Jose understood English.

In the future I would be more careful in the subjects I chose to discuss, what with our ever-present-understanding-English Jose by my side.

This conversation was upsetting me too. I wished that I could forget "any woman in her right mind would want a handsome airline Captain, even though he be my husband." I wished the whole stupid subject would float away, but it didn't. It set like cement and I thought about it all the time.

When Donald returned from B.A. and we were in our pillows he said, making conversation, "Sweetheart, what did you do while I was away?"

"Mostly I cried."

He said that was good. What else did I do?

"I played bridge each night with Jane and John Wagner and Colonel Braden."

"Braden, the Copper King himself, eh?"

"Si, Senor."

Silence for a while—"What else did you do besides cry while you played bridge with Copper King?"

"He took me to the races at Club Hippico. We spent Sunday together at the races."

"With John and Jane—and Braden?"

"No, just Colonel Braden and I. We spent the day together at Club Hippico. I won four thousand pesos."

Followed a long long silence. He said, "Aren't you going to ask me what I did in B.A.? B.A. is a wild place."

"No, I am not going to ask you what you did in B.A."

"Come on, ask me," he dared me. "I'll tell you the truth."

"Don't come limping back to me, confessing your sins. Go find a priest."

"I am not limping back! Are you going to ask me next week what I did in B.A.?"

"No. I am not going to ask you next week."

"You are not ever going to ask me?"

"No, Senor. I am not ever going to ask you."

"Can I depend on that?"

"Si, Senor, you can depend on that."

He said, "You know, you're a crazy wife!"

We lay very silent for a while. "What else did you do beside spend the day with Copper King?"

"Donald, your questions are becoming bothersome. Are you going to ask me every time you come home what I did while you were in B.A.?"

He said, angrily, he sure as hell was, and he sure as hell wanted to know more about Braden.

"Ah, honey, he's almost old enough to be my father. What's wrong with spending the day with a man who's almost old enough to be my father? I like young men."

"SO! You like young men!"

"I sure do!"

WHOOPS! I had said the wrong thing to this young man in my bed!

Four o'clock morning came too soon and the Panagra bus was waiting at the door for Donald who left without his breakfast. I sent him away with a smile on my

197

lips instead of with a sad tear on my cheek and I saw in his eyes doubt and concern as he grabbed his captain's cap and ran to the bus. Why was I smiling?

He returned from B.A. in anger and frustration and said he had not been able to think about one goddamned thing but me all the while he was in B.A. I was glad he had not been able to think about one goddamned thing but me. "Santiago is a hell of an unsafe place to leave a wife!" He lashed out at me and he carried his icy anger throughout the evening and to bed with us.

He fired gruelling questions at me and he was rough with me. I was glad he was furious and I said nothing to allay his anger. But this hour-on-hour tirade was getting out of hand and he was putting into words things that should not be put into words, for his thoughts were running wild. I saw that playing this game was a very fine way to lose a husband and I did not want to lose him. His hot fury was frightening me, so I told him the truth. There was no one, there never had been anyone, and there never would be anyone but him. I didn't have to tell him this because he already knew it.

Still too angry, he said, "I promise you I will blow the goddamned head off of any Senor who comes close!"

And I promised him that I would not share with any Senorita. He couldn't have both—it was Pilot's Choice! The penalties had been clearly defined. It was a very quiet and sleepless night.

I watched from my balcony at daylight, as Donald flew over our casa. I watched the Ford until the roar of three engines faded away. Again he was on his winged way to Buenos Aires!

And to what?

I sat with the icy wind in my face. Jose was most solicitous. He brought flowers for the balcony and he brought a mantilla for my shoulders. He thought I should come in out of the cold, though he apologized for suggesting. But I stayed on my balcony, and I asked Jose to bring me only a Martini for breakfast.

I watched, as the sun finally rose at mid-morning above the spires of the Andes. I watched, as the bread man came with his cartful of yesterday's loaves and buns. The vegetable wagon came at the slow pace of the oxen that drew it, and yellow-gold carrots with dew-dripping Kelly-green tops were carried, in bushel baskets, through the garden gates to the pony stable. The donkey cart from the flower mart arrived with its pink and yellow and lavender. The perfume of it was wind blown onto my balcony, and a sudden breeze was filled with pink petals. A beggar arrived for his daily pesos, and a peddler of saddle blankets called from atop his pile of woolen fringes.

Raphaela hung the wash in the empleados patio. I watched, almost smiling, as Madelyn galloped across the field on her pony Tony. Away she went, bare back and without bridle, for she and her pony had a perfect understanding. His tail, so carefully combed, streaked behind, as did her shining brown hair, and pony Tony's mane blew in Madelyn's face. Toto, the pup, determined to keep up, was doing so.

Some Senoras amigas passed on silver-bridled trotting horses, their black skirts sweeping from silver-studded sidesaddles. They waved gaily to me, calling that it was time to get up and not sit there in my nightgown. One laughingly chided, "Leave her alone! Captain Beatty was at home last night!"

Was he ever!

GATITO MAGNIFICO

Bred to the wilds Magnificat.

On his return from B.A. Donald brought me a box carefully tied up with pink and blue ribbons. It was a wiggly box, with holes in it. A kitten! The most adorable golden-furred, amber eyed Persian kitten. Immediately I named him "Magnificat" for truly he was a magnificent animal. I held him up to my cheek and he buzzed in my ear. He grabbed a claw full of my hair and tried to bite it. Donald said, "He is very gentle. I thought you might like him."

I did like him. I loved him. This soft and gentle little animal was now my prize possession.

Madelyn and all the empleados came quickly to see our new arrival.

"AH! Senora! Magnifico! Gatito magnifico!"

"Si, his name is Magnificat."

Donald told us how the kitten had passed out over

the "Hump" from lack of oxygen. Wild-eyed empleados gasped in anguish. He told how all the passengers had gone to sleep when the oxygen supply had given out, for a head wind had prolonged the passage. Then he told us how he had shared his own reserve of oxygen with the kitten who, seemingly a dead ball of fur, had suddenly started jumping and scratching to get out of the box, when he stuck his oxygen hose in it.

He told us how, in the down drafts, he had to hold Magnificat's box tightly between his knees, to keep it from hitting the ceiling of the cockpit. He thought maybe Magnificat had a cat fit when he turned oxygen into his box.

Madelyn laughed convulsively at her father's description, and she translated into Spanish as the empleados doubled up in hilarity. But I was not so sure I liked the idea of his sharing his precious oxygen with my cat.

He really was a magnificent animal, though he grew faster than any cat I ever saw. Within several weeks he was as large as Toto the Pup. Toto the Pup loved to maul Magnificat and Magnificat loved being mauled, though the cat was beginning to play rough, and the pup was not so aggressive any more. It was Magnificat that started the rough play, and Toto that began to withdraw, for it wasn't fun any longer.

The pony was becoming terrified when he saw Magnificat, for the cat would spring at him and hold on to Tony's neck with his teeth. Then one day I saw my cat spring at Toto and sink his teeth deep into his throat. And worse, one afternoon Madelyn came in screaming that Magnificat had eaten Flopsy, her rabbit. She said that Magnificat hid behind cortinas and would spring out at her, always springing for her throat. Immediately I told Donald.

One night Madelyn screamed, for Magnificat had

sprung into her bed with her and actually had bitten her on the throat. Donald came back into our room, got his always handy loaded pistol and said, coldly, "I must kill Magnificat. He is not full Persian, he is bred to the wild."

Madelyn and I both begged and pleaded and cried for another chance for Magnificat. But I knew Donald would shoot him. I held my hands over Madelyn's ears, hoping she would not hear. She continued to scream for reprieve as we both heard the shot.

Cold, cold violence everywhere! A land where even Persian kittens turn into vicious killers!

Donald was not moved. He cleaned his gun and put it back into the top drawer of his ropero. He said, "A cat was a lousy present."

On his return from B.A. when we stood together on my balcony alone in the moonlight, Donald handed me another box. It was not tied up with ribbons, neither did it have holes in it. It was long and narrow, of black velvet, from the Aveneda de Las Delicious. I pushed a very small white pearl bottom and the top sprung open to suddenly dazzle me with sparkling brightness. Diamonds for my wrist—diamonds of many sizes, twinkling and flashing blue sparks against black velvet. He said, "I thought you might like it."

I looked, unspeaking, at my lovely present. Diamonds, the emblem of love? Diamonds, so cold, so icy, so unmelting with warmth—so cutting. Why are diamonds the emblem of love when they themselves are all the things that love is not? I put it on and the moonlight struck it full on. Diamonds that last forever and forever. Diamonds born in the fires of first beginning on earth— enduring until the fiery end of all things. Forever, forever costly? Forever forever costly love? My beautiful bracelet. I put it on and I never took it off. I watched it sparkle in the moonlight that streaked across my bed.

From the Notes of Capt. Donald Beatty

. . . . . . **AFTER VISUAL OBSERVATION THAT THE PASS WAS CLEAR. . . . . ENTERING AND THEN———**

I found myself caged—blocked east and west by terrific snow whirls—north and south by the jagged walls of the gorge. I reported my altitude to Santiago flying around and around within the then clear portion of the Pass in an ever decreasing circle as the storm took over more and more of the canyon. My next radio report to Santiago reported that once again I was on "instruments." This I quickly followed with another report that we had crossed the Cumbre—on instruments—and had dropped down below the cloud level into the clear in the river valley on the Argentine side of the Cumbre. The clear atmosphere there was a most welcome sight, short lived, but most welcome. The eastern end of that canyon was blocked by the same storm which prevailed over the Cumbre and towards the west. . . continued here with Mt. Aconcagua 11 miles to the north and Tupengata to the south at a slightly greater distance—

Flight time for this transandean crossing had stretched to more than three times that of a normal trip. The separate high altitude oxygen supplies for passengers and pilots had both been exhausted by the time the violent up-drafts had forced the ship above 25,000-foot level.

Dear Reader:

Passengers didn't "go to sleep"; they passed out. It was passengers' choice; when crossing over the Hump of the High Andes, they could suck on the oxygen tube (that probably never had been washed) or they could pass out, due to lack of oxygen. Some preferred to pass out, for they would come back to consciousness at a lower altitude. Oxygen tubes were new contraptions and most passengers were afraid of them.

One feature writer, from the *Cosmopolitan* magazine, was sent to Chile to fly the Hump and write a feature story about the crossing. I will not call his name because he made us promise that we would never tell. He was young and muy macho and was convinced that he needed no pampering, such as sucking oxygen.

At first high altitude, his fountain pen blew up and squirted ink all over his note pad. It startled him and he dropped it. Then he leaned over to get a pencil from his brief case. Whammo! He was gone. He was out like a light, passed out. He was out until the plane landed at Los Cerillos. He never saw a peak of the Andes. He never felt an updraft or a down draft. He had nothing to write about. He would lose his job! Woe was he!

Donald invited him to our home for dinner and spread out hundreds of photographs he had taken of the High Andes. He described, so accurately, the sensations one feels in a crossing during a storm.

"Didn't anyone tell you," Donald asked, "that a fountain pen would blow up in the High Andes?"

"No! For God's sake, how could anyone but you know!"

The feature writer's story of the "Crossing over the Hump" was most dramatic, and accurate. He sent Donald an edition of the magazine that featured it, and he included a copy of a congratulatory letter from his superior, who wrote, "I was THERE!"

CRASH!

With Donald flying the search flights, and also the scheduled flights over the Hump to B.A., Panagra needed another pilot. It was then that Sam Eisenman came to Chile. Sam was a young man with a beautiful wife, Berta. They had been married only a short time, and coming to Chile was a honeymoon. Berta was a brunette and looked so much a part of Chilean society, for she was tall and slender. Sam was the stock German type, with sandy hair, a lot of it. They were in love.

But Berta had a great and uncontrollable premonition of danger, not uncommon among pilots' wives. Being with her sometimes upset me, for I did not care to talk about such things, not even to think of such things. A pilot's wife should put such things out of her mind altogether. But Berta could not.

Donald was flying the regular schedule over the Hump, with Sam as co-pilot, so that he could accumulate sufficient hours to be checked out as pilot. Berta and I spent most of our time together when our husbands were away, for we had become best friends. I tried to help her, as others had helped me, to get settled and to make friends, but she was too much in love to take interest in anything but the Ford that brought Sam back to her.

Her premonition of disaster was growing instead of subsiding. I felt that I should do something to break this terrible spell. But what! Actually I was losing patience with her for she had married a pilot. She should adjust. Finally Sam was checked out. With Sam himself flying the Ford she might feel better about it. She did feel better and all of us were relieved.

Berta was a great one to sew and I, more to have company than to sew, was spending the day with her. Both our husbands were in the High Andes, both due in that afternoon. We were happy as we sat by the fire and talked and sewed and drank tea that the maid brought. But Berta was sorry she and Sam had come to Chile. There was nothing about Chile that she liked. There was violence everywhere that frightened her and she was dreadfully nervous all the time. She wanted to go home.

I pointed out that our husbands loved this violence. They loved every minute of their flying in the High Andes with its storms. But Bertha loathed flying. She wished with all her heart that they had not come to Santiago.

I said, "Come on, honey, come on. Let's go to my casa and have dinner together. Sam and Donald can come on the Panagra bus for they will be getting in about the same time. We can have dinner together, all four of us."

"I would like that. I hate my cook! Neither Sam nor I can eat anything she cooks. We detest Chilean food."

"Jose will find you another cook. I will speak to him."

We drove to my casa and Jose had Martinis waiting for us, as was his custom.

The phone rang and it was Anabel. Smitty and Anabel were coming over to visit. They called to be sure we were there. "Great! Both Berta and I are here. Sam and Donald are coming on the Panagra bus. Come on over. Stay for dinner.''

Unannounced, John and Jane Wagner dropped in to visit. Then Byron and Sue Rickards, then our sweet Chilean friend, Lolla. Jose brought drinks, but there was a strange something everywhere, like an icy wind coming back at us from the Andes.

I asked, ''What is this, old home week, a surprise party? Whose birthday? Berta, is this your birthday?''

She laughed and said, ''No.''

The silence was becoming stuffed with tension. I said, ''Smitty, what goes on?''

He waited an eternity, then he said, ''There has been an accident.''

I looked at Berta and we both blanched. ''What sort of accident?''

Smitty said, ''The weather has closed in completely. Both Sam's and Donald's Fords are out of communication. One of them is reported down. That is all we know.''

It was the first time around for Berta and for me. This sort of news—we really did not understand what it meant.

Byron Rickards was on the phone, talking with Los Cerrillos. When he returned to the living room we jumped at him. ''Was there any further news!''

Byron stood there, silent, very silent. He said nothing. Oh Dear God! It was bad news! All of us could feel it, all of us knew.

Byron said, trying to cushion the blow, ''Only one plane has been spotted. There is reason to hope that the other plane still is in the air, but the storm is violent.''

Oh Dear God! There could be two planes down! Both Sam and Donald could be down in the High Andes! But only one had been spotted! Byron was lying! He knew more. But did I want to know more? Panic seized Berta and me as we stood together.

Anabel asked, "Have they heard anything more about the plane that is down? Where is it? What more do they know?"

"Nothing more, only that one plane has been spotted."

Byron was lying and all of us knew he was keeping something from us. "Byron, tell me! I have to know. What are you waiting for? Tell me!"

He said, quietly, "One plane has been spotted in Lake Junin. There can be no survivors."

I could not look at Berta. I wanted her out of my life and I wished with all my heart that she would go away, for it had to be her husband and not mine in that wreck with no survivors. I prayed that it was Sam and not Donald. But it was too late to pray. It was all over. In one flash, it was all over.

I left the room. I went to the other end of the house, for I had to get away from everyone. But there was no place to get away, for at the other end of the house the empleados were weeping and praying and crossing themselves. I screamed at them, "Everybody go away! Jose, get them out of here! I have to be alone!"

Byron came to me and said quietly, "We think Donald is still in the air. We are not sure, but we think so."

They were not sure! Oh Dear God! It was BOTH of them!

Smitty and Anabel came to me and Smitty put his big arms around me, but it was of no comfort. He said, "Come on back to the living room. Don't stay out here by yourself."

How could I go back? Berta was the last person on earth I wanted to see. But I went back. As I came into the living room she ran to me and grabbed my hand. We stood together, welded to our panic. All was deadly quiet. Then I heard the weird wailing of the caged animals in the zoo atop Mt. San Cristobal, this strange forerunner of a temblor, for the caged animals knew before we that the earth would shake. Their wailing reached a high pitch, then the now-familiar-to-me subcontra rumble beneath the earth began to be audible. The empleados screamed "TEMBLOR!" and streaked from the house. The house began to shake, glass in the lava-plata fell and broke. Everyone moved against a door jamb as the earthquake progressed, everyone but Berta and me. We stood together in our double shock, in the center of the room, until Smitty came and made us move under an archway into the hall.

The earthquake progressed in intensity. A window swung open, the ceiling cracked and sifted white plaster on the floor. A mirror fell from the wall and broke. The house shook violently with ever growing intensity. Berta screamed, "It is shaking Sam out of my life!"

It was a hard shake and a long shake. It seemed to last forever.

But little by little the motion slowed, little by little the caged animals in the zoo stopped wailing, little by little drums stopped beating. The freight train that ran over us had passed. The servants returned to the house, still wringing their hands and praying.

The phone rang and both Berta and I screamed. Byron answered it, talked a brief minute to Los Cerrillos, then he came and stood in archway. He looked at me with a faint smile that almost said Donald was still in the air. Berta saw his smile. She turned on me, grabbed me by the shoulders and shook me. "Tell me!" she screamed. "Tell me! I have to know! Tell me it isn't Sam!"

Jane and Sue took Berta out of the room, trying in some way to comfort her. "Tell me!" she continued to scream. "Tell me it isn't Sam!"

But, yes, it was Sam. For Captain Beatty, in a badly storm-damaged Ford, with bruised and frightened passengers, had just landed in Los Cerrillos.

Berta stayed with us. It was heartbreak time.

She said, "I am not pregnant. If only I were! If only I had something of Sam's to take home with me! I have nothing."

I helped her pack to go home. "Berta, what shall I do with this closet full of Sam's clothes?"

"Don't touch them!" she screamed at me. "Don't touch them!"

She ran to the closet and buried her face in Sam's clothes, and she sobbed. I sat on the side of the bed, then I buried my face in a pillow. I made no attempt to comfort her, for she was far beyond comforting.

It was a long time before her spasm of grief subsided, but finally it spent itself. In quiet exhaustion she said again, "Don't touch Sam's clothes. They will hang right there forever, just as he left them. I will leave with nothing. I came with everything! Oh, God! Why did we come!" She sobbed.

Another spasm of grief. I closed the closet, and I stopped packing her things, for I knew that she would leave, as she said, with nothing.

"I want Donald to take me out of this hell tomorrow. I wish he could fly me all the way home to Shreveport."

The next day Donald flew her to Antafogasta, the northernmost station of the Southern Division of Panagra.

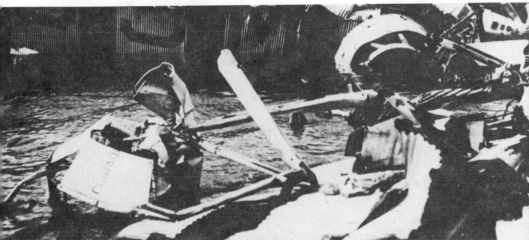

The wreckage of Sam's tri-motored Ford was spotted in Lake Junin. There could be no survivors.

MAC AND EVELYN

We wondered who would take Sam Eisenman's place. Andean pilots were hard to come by and there were no co-pilots ready to be checked out as captain. Smitty would cable Captain MacMillan, who was in the States on three-months vacation, to see if he would return to Santiago early. Yes, Mac would fly back at once. His wife Evelyn and their little daughter would come later by Grace Line cruise to Panama. She would fly from Panama to Santiago.

Mac arrived within the week. He was happy to return and rearing to get back into the left side of the cockpit, for vacationing was a bore. He preferred flying to any other thing on earth and as far as he was concerned if he never took another vacation it was O.K. Mac was just like all the Andean Pilots, they wanted nothing more than to fly the High Andes. They wanted no vacation.

Mac was a stocky young man in his late twenties. He was strong and heavyset. One never would doubt that he could handle a Ford in the High Andes. He had big hands that easily spread three throttles. And he had a look in his eyes that Andean Pilots had.

He and Evelyn had been married for years, and they

took each other casually. But Mac was impatient for her to
arrive. He missed her.

"You'll love Evelyn," Anabel said to me. "She is so
much fun, so wacky. I can't wait to hear her new jokes."

"Is she tall, short, brunette, blond?"

"Brunette, pretty. You should hear her jokes!"

"Shocking?"

"I'll say! But funny. She's a scream. You'll love
Evelyn." Evelyn was just what I needed, for to laugh came
hard just now.

Evelyn was due in today and all the Panagra pilots
and their wives had gone to Los Cerrillos to meet her.
Happy times! Evelyn was coming! But she wasn't on the
plane, although her name was on the passenger list.

Mac walked around, wondering what had happened
to her, when suddenly a gorgeous platinum blond, looking
like Jean Harlow, threw her arms around the startled Mac.
It was Evelyn! Gorgeous platinum blond Evelyn, with her
little daughter also platinum blonded.

Evelyn was the first platinum blond in Santiago and,
everywhere she went, she created a sensation. Mac was
elated. He had a brand new Senora. Instead of a brunette
Senora he now had a gorgeous platinum blond Senora!
And I was to learn that those two were hard to keep up
with. Just as Anabel had said, they kept all of Panagra
perpetually laughing and shocked.

The gang of us went to the Union Club for dinner
that night. I watched in awe and disbelief as Chilean men,
old friends of Mac's, threw big masculine arms around
him and hugged him. Some of them kissed him. I never
had seen men hug and kiss each other. But this was the "El
Braso," an old Spanish Custom. I couldn't help but wonder what would happen if a man threw his arms around
Donald and kissed him. Old Spanish Custom or not, we
had an Old Alabama Custom. Should a man throw his

arms around Donald and kiss him, I believe Donald would knock him cold.

With Berta gone I had to look for another close friend. Maybe this glamorous, happy, wacky Jean Harlow Evelyn would become my friend.

REVOLUTION: ARMY VS. AIR FORCE

From our first meeting Evelyn and I liked each other. Immediately we became best friends.

She said, "Has there been a revolution lately?"

"There is one going on now. They say the Chilean Army is fighting the Chilean Air Force. Donald thinks I should stay in mi casa."

"Getting more and more like a Chilean Senor? Thinks his Senora should stay home all the time?"

"How did you know?"

The next week, when Donald and Mac were in B.A., Evelyn and I went to the Aveneda de Las Delicious to watch the Carabineros ride their beautiful horses, in patrolling the streets of Santiago, in holding down the revolution. It was a spectacular sight to see them come, hundreds of them, mounted on their sleek, trotting, silver-bridled horses. They came in perfect formation, four abreast, with pennants fluttering atop ten-foot-long, steel-bayonet-tipped lancetas.

The Carabineros were arresting officers, judges, executioners, all in one. They kept the peace, for when they lowered their ten-foot-long lancetas, tipped with steel bayonets and said, MOVE! everyone moved, but pronto.

Once, when Evelyn and I were watching this spectacular patrol, the crowd stood too close to the edge of the sidewalk and the Carabinero commanded, MOVE BACK! He only told us once, then he took out after us, on his horse, with lanceta lowered. Evelyn and I ran into the Hotel Crillon, fled to the tea room on the mezzanine. But the Carabinero followed us, and rode his horse up the wide red-carpeted staircase. Evelyn and I fled further, to a room marked URINARIO. It turned out to be the urinario for Senores.

We told no one.

Then one afternoon when Evelyn and I drove to Los Cerrillos to meet Donald and Mac, who were coming in from Montevideo in the Fairchild, I saw soldiers crouched down in the ditch beside the road. I said, "Evelyn, soldiers are lying in the ditch on my side of the road." She slowed down, almost to a stop, and stuck her head out of the window to see. Then she turned her puzzled wide brown eyes to me and said, "Soldiers are lying in the ditch on my side of the road, too. Why do you suppose they do that?" I couldn't guess why but there was no doubt that they did, for there were hundreds of them crouched so low that only their hunched backs were showing.

Suddenly several soldiers scrambled out of the ditch and blocked the road in front of us with their rifles. One stood, spraddle-legged, directly in front of our car, rifle with bayonet pointed at us. He demanded, in fierce language, HALT! Then he lowered his rifle and all of them waved frantically for us to go back. GO BACK! GO BACK! SENORITAS, GO BACK! But it was too late. The revolution exploded into machine gun fire as hundreds of soldiers jumped out of the ditches and blasted at a Chilean Air Force plane that was coming in for a landing.

Evelyn screamed above the noise of battle, "The Chilean Army is fighting the Chilean Air Force, just like Mac said. Let's stay and watch." I nodded "Si" for the soldiers were not shooting in our direction, they were shooting in the opposite direction and they had forgotten all about us.

The Air Force plane, trying to dodge gun fire, swooped low, but too low. One wing struck the ground. The plane rolled over, crashed in the field immediately behind the Panagra hangar and burst into flames. Bullets riddled the fallen plane and some hit the Panagra hangar, knocking out windows. A terrified Panagra mechanic dashed from the hangar, ran out into the field, yanked off his only garment, a white coverall, and ran, stark naked, waving his coverall over his head, his white flag of surrender. Machine guns continued to pump round after round of ammunition as Panagra mechanics fled from the building and flattened themselves on the tarmac.

We saw Donald and Mac coming in for a landing. They were too low to turn and go back. We watched the Fairchild go into a vertical slip, straight to the ground and squash to a landing. Donald and Mac jumped out, ran from the plane, and flattened on the tarmac, along with the Panagra mechanics, who had beat them to this safety. Finally the firing ceased and Army soldiers swarmed to the field behind the Panagra hangar to watch the twisted, broken, flaming plane, along with its pilot, burn to ashes.

The battle was over. The Chilean Army had won. The Chilean Air Force had lost.

Donald and Mac lay still for a while, then they got up, shook themselves a bit, and walked to the car. Our husbands were mad with us. They wished we would stay out of the revolution for "we'd get killed, sure as hell!"

NEW YEAR'S DAY
UNDER THE SOUTHERN
CROSS

It was Christmas in Chile, Christmas 1932. This silly, summertime, flower-blooming Christmas! This crazy upside-down world below the Equator! Better still, it soon would be New Year's Day! That was the BIG DAY of all the year, and the New Year's Day Fox Hunt in Santiago was the greatest social affair in all Chile. This fabulous Fox Hunt was an uninterrupted twenty-four hour Fiesta. It began at the Estancia of Senor Garcia Ganzales for breakfast and for the start of the Hunt. Then it progressed to the Estancia of Don Fernandez to welcome back the hunters, to dine and dance under the stars until sunrise, then to partake of "desayuno" on the morning of January second. Twenty-four hours of unbelievably elegant Fiesta to welcome in the New Year, and speed it on its way! New Year's Day in Chile, 1933!

An invitation to this twenty-four hour Fiesta was a most coveted prize, and each year the Panagra captains and their Senoras were included in this fabulous affair. Mac and Evelyn and Donald and I would go together.

About nine o'clock in the morning of New Year's Day we arrived at the Estancia of Senor Ganzales. The courtyard was filled with guests and horses. The most

218

beautiful horses! Those horses entered in the Hunt had their tails and manes intricately braided with silver canchos plaited into the braids. Those horses not entered in the Hunt were heavily leadened with silver-studded saddles and their shampooed and combed tails swept the ground. The horses waited impatiently, so beautifully trained to prance and champ at the bit. A magnificent stallion, completely unadorned, was seen in the background, being shown by two grooms who held him firmly in restraint.

Red coated hunters were everywhere, and velvet coated grooms handled the hounds. Somewhere in el campo the Fox had been set free, and the hunters waited and preened themselves until time to take up the Chase. La Senora Ganzales appeared in her sweeping train-like black divided skirt. She mounted her steed, rode about among her guests, laughing and talking in her most elegant manner.

It wasn't time to begin the Chase, for breakfast came first. We were seated, hundreds of us. For three hours we were served from silver trays so large and heavy that it took two empleados to carry each tray. There seemed to be Kings and Queens, Lords and Ladies—and ALL THE KING'S HORSES!

Finally the Chase began, just as it did in a Samuel Goldwyn Mayer production. A horn sounded, hounds strained at their leashes, horses reared. THEY WERE OFF! Down the campo, jumping dry walls, jumping eseacuas, jumping low primly cut hedges.

I thought that I must have been watching a movie, else time had gone mad. For this had to be 1833. This could not be 1933!

We followed the guests to the Estancia of Don Fernandez to celebrate the Finish of the Hunt and to dance and dine away the year. The estancia of Don Fernandez was the most renowned estancia in Chile. The main casa spread, seemingly over acres of land, and the courtyard was tremendous. The gardens had no beginning and no ending. Arbours were everywhere, covered with wisteria-like blossoms. Trees hung heavy with cherries and tables were spread, in the sun and in the shade, each guest having his preference.

And hammocks! Who ever saw so many hammocks! They hung between cherry trees, seemingly secretly, in a garden of their own. The hammocks were multicolored, hand woven, with lace-like fringes, every color of the Chilean Rainbow. They swung quietly, casually, empty. They swished a bit in the afternoon breeze, playfully inviting guests to a lazy siesta.

The hunters, in not at all mussed red coats, returned from the Chase. A fox tail was hung, still dripping with blood. Dogs were barely under control and horses were white with sweat. Laughter and wine were all around. And before the sun went down the tables began to fill, and fine food was passed. This dinner was to last for hours, or for all night, should one care to sit at the tables with good wines and uproarious laughter.

The orchestra had arrived, and a small dance floor had been set up in the garden. But the hunters themselves were the attraction. They were the honored guests of the evening, and they were enjoying their position of distinction. Senores talked Men's Talk in wisecracks and undertones. Donald and Mac were completely focused to this Men's World. Evelyn and I, being apart from such things, not allowed to hear such talk, preferred to dance. So, with our more than willing Chilean escorts, we left the table for the dance floor. FIESTA! FIESTA!

I was, of course, wearing my Chilean corset and my Chilean crocheted brassiere. I had avoided eating the tremendous dinner from necessity, for there was no room within the confines of my corset for anything other than me. But I looked like a respectable Senora is supposed to look. That was what mattered most to me, for I was a pilot's wife and I wanted to be completely proper. Tonight, too, I would find out if Chilean men would dance with me, now that I was wearing a corset.

Stars spread the sky. The Southern Cross besplendored, replacing the Big Dipper that I knew so well and missed so much.

My dance partner was erect, unbending, definitely from the elite. Instinctively I knew he was an important Senor. I must be very careful. I must follow the customs of his country. His very dark hair was a bit longer than American men wore their hair. His dinner jacket was different from the white mess jackets worn by Panagra pilots, his being of a dark purple, trimmed in velvet. He was perfectly schooled in formal behavior, his attention was nowhere except with me.

He danced a different Tango from the one I had known, for his Tango had something to do with the eyes. Heels and eyes were riveted to the same beat and I followed his Tango through his eyes, for the rhythm was there. It was a fun way to dance. I had thought one felt rhythm-beat best when one danced cheek to cheek with one's eyes closed. It was not true. One hears the beat more distinctly when one dances not so close, and with one's heels on the floor, with one's eyes wide open. Eyes wide open seemed a bit too fun loving if not brazen, but a tango with heels clicking and with eyes wide open is definitely delightful.

It reminded me of a Rumba I learned to dance—so long ago in San Julian. Fragments of memories fluttered like confetti around me. Tango eyes—Rumba eyes—eyes under the Big Dipper—eyes under the Southern Cross—

My Tango partner suggested we sit awhile—in a hammock? That sounded nice, though to me it sounded a bit irregular. But I must not offend. I must follow the New

Year's Custom.

I looked, and one of the hammocks was occupied. A Senorita was lying there, serenely. Her lacy skirt spilled from one side of the hammock and fell in a puddle of ruffles on the grass. I adored the way she looked. Her partner sat beside her on a low carved bench. This was such a lovely custom, the Senorita lying so quietly in a hammock while her Senor sat beside her on a low carved bench. I'd follow this custom and do precisely as the Senora was doing. My lacy skirt would spill from one side of the hammock and look just as lovely as hers. My Senor too would sit beside me on a low carved bench and occasionally swing my hammock. This was a dreamy way to spend the New Year's Day, 1933. Why would Donald and Mac choose to talk "Airplanes" on a night like this!

Lanterns with candles continued to wink knowingly in the garden as I lay in my hammock. My Senor and I discussed, as best we could across a language barrier, stars and flowers and trees that hung heavy with cherries. It was then, when I mentioned cherries, that he got up from his carved bench and brought me one, just one, huge and ripe and juicy.

The Senor asked me most pleasantly, and most formally, if he might get in the hammock with me. I was completely surprised and shocked. I looked at the other hammocks. True, some hammocks had two occupants. Senoritas lay quietly and sedately talking with their partners. Their partners had one foot on the ground, rhythmically making the hammocks rock. I wondered if one foot on the ground was a rule in Chile. It was a good rule. We did not have that rule in Alabama.

But I really was shocked. I was not ready for this two-in-a-hammock New Year's Day, even with Senor's one foot on the ground. I was shocked! How did Senoritas get out of hammocks? I looked and saw that Senoritas were not getting out of hammocks. They seemed quite content where they were.

Senor asked again, most pleasantly, most formally, if he might get in my hammock. I said, "Pardon, Senor, What did you say? I didn't understand. My Spanish is poor."

He was most affably polite and restrained. He dropped the subject—let it alone for the time being.

I thought this must be some sort of Chilean New Year's Day game that I should play. But it was a new game to me and I didn't know how to handle it. I didn't know the rules. My Spanish guidebook had made no mention of hammocks. This Chilean game was brand new to me and I could see in the Senor's eyes that he was looking for a brand new game for himself, like maybe a pilot's wife. It was a silly little game but it might be fun to play, since I held all the cards. I thought the Senor could not possibly get in my hammock, unless I let him. He could not possibly win.

We discussed the firmament, the Southern Cross. I said that I missed the Big Dipper, that the night sky seemed strange and empty without it. I missed the horizon too, for in all directions in Santiago the horizon was blocked out by the Andes. I was vaguely annoyed that he was amused by my confusion and my evasion of his subject. I was doubly annoyed for having put myself at so great a disadvantage, what with swinging so elegantly in this confounded hammock.

Just as I thought he would, he moved, with pleasant and unabrasive self-confidence, quietly back to his subject, he wanted to get in my hammock. This time he used a different and more simple vocabulary. Surely I could understand.

He gestured to the pink hammock as translation of what he had in mind. I knew exactly what he had in mind, for two-in-a-hammock in Chile was precisely the same as two-in-a-hammock in Alabama. I noticed that the Senorita in the pink hammock was not so formal as the Senoritas in the other hammocks. And if her Senor was not careful he was going to turn over the pink hammock, for he had no foot on the ground.

He wanted to get in my hammock. I was unwilling but I did not know the Spanish word for unwilling. The language gap between us was a terrible disadvantage for me, for I knew no Spanish words of fine points and vague meanings. I knew only basic vocabulary and at a time like this there was no place for basic vocabulary such as, "Si, Senor" or "No, Senor". After all, who was this Senor? One I must not offend? I said nothing.

Continuing where he left off, he returned smoothly and precisely and with charm back to his subject. But I noted that the Senor also was at a disadvantage. He was annoyed with his own vocabulary for basic Spanish was too clumsy for his purpose. This most handsome man definitely was not a clumsy Senor.

I was not interested in his age-old argument but I was becoming interested in his approach to it for I never had heard it in Spanish, basic Spanish.

His approach to it now was through a deft use of reassurance. "Senorita," he explained, "this is the New Year's Day custom in Chile. Do you not have such a custom in the United States?"

This approach quietly maneuvered me into reflections upon New Year's Eve in Alabama, when, at the stroke of New Year's Day, the lights went out on the ballroom floor, and they stayed out for a long time, sometimes even longer than that. What was so different between a kiss on the ballroom floor, with all the lights out, and a kiss in a hammock with the lanterns winking? But I did not believe this was a Chilean New Year's custom. It was only an innovation for those guests who did not care to follow the hounds.

I looked into his fun-promising eyes, and I knew that I was pitted against a champion. Had I been wrong when I thought he could not win?

The sheer audacity of this Senor was attractive to me. Some day an angry husband might blow off his head. Was he not aware of this? Suddenly I remembered an angry husband who had most bluntly promised me that he would indeed blow off the God damned head of such a Senor. I was afraid. And that was good, because my fear and my fear alone was keeping this Senor and his Chilean Custom out of my hammock.

"Do you not have such a custom in the United States?" he put in the follow-up.

Reluctantly I told him that in Alabama it was a most rigid ground rule to stay out of hammocks, especially on New Year's Day. Senor was most unhappy with my Alabama ground rule.

Suddenly there was a squeal and a thump. The pink hammock had turned over, just as I thought it would. Senor said, "Desmanado." I said, "Si, clumsy."

There was no language barrier to our laughter, for both of us knew why the pink hammock had turned over. This was a pleasant way out of a showdown, for both of us. Stifling his laughter, he took both my hands and pulled me up from the hammock, and with mock pleading, he said, "Senorita from Alabama, please, may I dance with you?" With both feet on the ground and still laughing, I answered in my basic Spanish, "Si, Senor!"

Had I won?

It was just after New Year's Day when Donald called me one afternoon from Los Cerrillos. He hesitated a minute, then asked if I could go to Evelyn, or perhaps bring her to our house. "Why? are we going to the Union Club tonight?'' That sounded nice. Mac was coming in this afternoon.

"No, not the Union Club. Can you go stay with Evelyn? Bring her and the little girl to our house to spend the night.'' A sudden freeze hit my bloodstream. Could I go stay with Evelyn—bring her and her little girl to spend the night!

Donald said he would be home soon. John and Jane Wagner and Byron and Sue Rickards, and Smitty and Anabel would be there; he was calling them.

Dear God! Not Mac! Not another crash! Por Dios!

Donald waited for the blow to penetrate, and for him to fashion the words that would not come. But, yes, it was Mac. For Captain MacMillan too had been helplessly caught in the turbulence of the High Andes, and had been flung into the downdraft that roared down the glacier. The Ford had been sucked into this mighty undertow and ground to pieces on the icy slopes of Aconcagua. Pieces of the Ford were seen scattered in the crevasse. There could be no survivors.

Heartbreak, greater than anyone can imagine. Packing-to-go-home-alone-heartbreak! Before the packing was done, there was another crash. Captain McMickle crashed out of Lima. There were no survivors. And there was still another. Captain Sheets had disappeared. The search for him and his passengers had begun. The wives of the remaining pilots were going to pieces. There was nothing in Chile but terror.

Search for the *San Jose* continued and, with it, the search for some clue by which downdrafts could be predicted. Donald would fly to exact locations in the Andes, to check turbulence at different times of day, in varying weather conditions, always looking for patterns. There were a few findings that seemed to denote a slight possibility of constancy, but mostly the findings bore out, rather conclusively, that total unpredictability was the perpetual pattern in the violence of the High Andes.

I knew so well the gamble he continuously took. What chance on earth did he have of always winning? I knew, if he ever missed a calculation, he would be down forever. And this hellish discordant refrain kept coming back at me, like a chorus repeating itself after each stanza, "Down forever and forever, and forever, and forever." I could not close my ears to it, for it was not with my ears that I heard it.

Although he was exhausted with handling so many extra hours, when we were in our pillows, he tried to make light of it all.

"You'll never guess what happened to me today in Uspallata Pass."

"What?"

"Crates of lobsters broke open, and hundreds of the critters crawled all over me." He guffawed, remembering it.

He was flying the "Lobster Special." The lobsters came from Robinson Crusoe Island, out in the Pacific, and regularly scheduled flights delivered them to exclusive restaurants in B.A. Hundreds of them, alive and crated, were packed in the Fairchild, and the pilot was a one-man crew, being also navigator and radio man, for every available inch of space was needed for lobsters.

"Old Razor Back was so tail heavy with lobsters that I had to wedge my arm against the stick to hold it in the air. Then I hit a downdraft and several crates split open." He guffawed again. "The things crawled all over me, over my head, hung on to my goggles, I couldn't see. There I was, in the turbulence of Uspallata, couldn't turn loose the stick for a second!" I tried to laugh, but there was nothing funny anywhere. There was only fear.

I turned madly to my Steinway and practiced furiously for hours on end each day he was flying. Chilean ladies of the Music Club invited me to give a concert, and I foolishly accepted. On the stage I modulated into the wrong key, smudged notes in my chords, tightened, came apart before my final number, and left the stage in tears. They understood and tried to comfort me, explaining to each other, "Captain Beatty is flying the High Andes today."

Smitty suggested Donald and I go to B.A. for a short vacation. After all, Donald never had taken a vacation, not even for a week. And I never had flown across the HUMP. Maybe, if I flew over those magnificent peaks, I would have a different outlook.

Donald wanted to fly me across the Hump to B.A. He himself wanted to show me, for the first time, his beloved Andes. He would show me Aconcagua. He would show me Los Penitentes and The Christ of the Andes. He would fly me beyond Uspallata, over the vast ice lands. He would fly low over the Pampa and chase ostriches. We would go to La Tabarisse, in B.A. We would hit the Hot Spots. We would play roulette in Monte, and he would show me his system that always won blue pearl 1,000 peso chips.

This crazy Captain Beatty! He actually loved this wild and terrifying land!

As we flew over the staggering brilliance of the High Andes that sparkled in dazzling white, this whitest of all earthly white, I knew it truly was a FOREVER AND FOREVER LAND. It was FOREVER, FOREVER AND FOREVER A RHAPSODY IN ICE.

THE *SAN JOSE* FOUND

Our vacation lasted but a day, for we were awakened in our most luxurious resort hotel, Parque in Montevideo, Uruguay by a call from Smitty in Santiago. Donald was to return at once, for the *San Jose* had been found.

Gold prospectors, digging for the "Mother lode" in the foot hills of the Andes, had found part of a copper oil line. WHAT HAD THEY FOUND? They found other parts of a motor in surrounding melting snow and ice. Little by little ice-encrusted parts led to the wreckage.

The *San Jose* lay where, for two years, it had been completely blanketed and hidden, in hundreds of feet of snow and ice. It lay still entombed within the ice mausoleum that Jupiter Rex had erected over his victim.

But the Sun God had turned the heat of his fury upon the sepulcher, slowly melting it away, slowing exhuming, slowly unshrouding the twisted steel skeleton.

The Sun God had found the *San Jose*.

With the *San Jose* found, and the search terminated, there was a reorganization of personnel throughout Panagra. Pilots were being relocated, new pilots were being brought in from the States, and the manager of the Southern Division, John Shannon, was being transferred to the New York office. Donald was being transferred to Panama, where he would become manager of the Northern Division of Panagra. This transfer moved him into international airline management.

It was imperative that he leave at once. Madelyn and I could come later, by cruise ship, if we cared. Why wait! What was there to wait for? Madelyn and I would leave immediately, with Donald.

Packing was simple. I gave away almost all that we had. We would leave as we had come, with no baggage. The pets were given to eager children; my empleados were in great demand. Mrs. Burgan was returning to her husband in Tumaco; Jose was going with the American Embassy, for he understood English.

I longed to hug and kiss them goodby, but it was not the custom to do so. My empleados stood, stiffly in line, according to their social order, and they bowed a formal, "Adios."

Truly this was "Adios," forever and forever. But Madelyn and I could not bring ourselves to say, "Adios." We said instead, "Hasta Luego" (for a little while). Madelyn was crying. So were all my empleados. She pleaded with Jose to take good care of her animals, especially her pony Tony and Toto the Pup. My empleados stood, in uncontrolled weeping, saying through their tears, "Hasta Luego, Senora. Hasta Luego, Senorita Madelyn."

Chile now truly would be a NEVER NEVER land for me, for NEVER NEVER would I, at daybreak, wave from my balcony to a Fairchild or to a Ford that blew me a kiss and continued its flight into the sunrise.

I felt no gladness. I felt no sadness. I felt nothing but the leaving itself. For Donald was LEAVING! LEAVING ALIVE! He was not remaining FOREVER, FOREVER buried in the snows of the High Andes.

I thanked my God!

From the Notes of Capt. Donald Beatty

It would be difficult to record, in chronological order, the many details of each of the 120-odd search flights I piloted before we finally located the wreckage of the *San Jose*. I suppose that the best manner of describing the usual flight would be in the form of a composite . . . a recapitulation from my flight log book covering a typical search flight. Clear air turbulence was ever present, the severe low temperatures over the glaciers and snow fields at the high altitudes could always be depended upon. Last but far from least was the difficulty in just remaining alert to the requirements at hand—the low cabin temperatures (my chronometer wrist watch would frequently stop during a flight—the small amount of lubricant would more-or-less solidify and freeze its movements) and oxygen deficiency had a most telling effect upon alertness. Many times during search flights I've observed the outside air temperature gauge to register more than minus 60 degrees Fahrenheit—the indicating thermometer needle resting against the stop-pin and apparently almost bending to register even a lower temperature!

As had frequently occurred in the past, I began each search flight at dawn. The takeoff would always be without incident from the sod-covered Los Cerrillos airfield which served Santiago, Chile as an airport. I would follow a more-or-less routine by holding the aircraft in a steep climbing attitude on a northeasterly heading towards Los Andes, a small town in the foothills of the Andes at the Chilean entrance to the 140-mile long Uspallata Pass through the mountains separating Chile and Argentina. The Pass was the "dividing line" or bench mark as the individual search flight was programmed by me to be conducted either to the north or south of that line.

The flight was a repetition of many I had undertaken over a period of more than seventeen months. Each time I believed, as did my radio operator and the observer/cameraman, that on that particular occasion the wreckage of the lost airliner *San Jose* would be spotted. The search area was large, doubly so when the high altitude and rough terrain of the area was taken into consideration. It covered more than 30,000 square miles of jagged, vertically walled gorges, peaks and dry river canyons, glaciers and snow fields of the highest ranges of the Andes mountains. On a horizontal scale the area stretched for more than 200 miles north and south and somewhat less east and west. A large portion of it had never been explored even from the air nor had human eyes previously viewed it.

It may be asked "why did the search flight always begin at dawn?" The reason was a practical one. From data collected beginning with my first such flight I soon detected a pattern which indicated, among other things, that clear air turbulence over the Andes was at a minimum at dawn. The increasing sun heat with advancing daylight hours appeared to be a major catalyst which added greatly to the severe air invection eddies. The high velocity westerly winds usually encountered at the upper altitudes during the daylight hours were also minimal during the early pre-dawn period. As the day progressed so did the westerly winds which, upon encountering the high Andes, were deflected upward in irregular columns of tumbling, turbulent

forces. The persistent high-altitude clear-air turbulence resulting from such conditions happens to
be the most universal characteristic of the high
Andes together with the perpetual glaciers, jagged,
granite peaks, and instantaneous snow storms
which sometimes do last for weeks! Westerly
winds, increasing as the day advances, shriek out of
control as they comb through the crests of the peaks
then descend into the gorges and dry river canyons
of the mountains, gathering strength in a howling
and destructive force. Because of the data which I
had collected beginning with my first search flight,
transandean flights were subsequently re-
scheduled in-so-far as was possible to early morning
hours as an aid towards safety of flight and to the
comfort of passengers and crew of the scheduled
airline transandean operation.

No search flight could, by any stretch of the im-
agination, be characterized as a "joy ride."
Emergency situations were always injected. Extremely severe clear-air turbulence, CAT, was
always there and on several occasions rolled the aircraft I was flying over on its back. On at least three
other engraved memories in my "mental file" the
lead weight at the end of the trailing radio antenna
(about 63-feet long) was dragged off by contact with
the earth—glacier or mountain top—resulting from
encountering a severe but invisible down-draft
which forced the aircraft within feet of the earth.
Once or twice the trailing antenna was wrapped
around the fuselage of the aircraft as it rolled
over—it remained there until the landing back at Los
Cerrillos airfield!

The prevailing weather condition in the mountain pass was unknown to Captain Robinson at the

time of his mid-winter takeoff from Santiago. The important meteorological station had not yet been installed near the statue of Christus of the Andes at the Cumbre. His visual observation from Los Cerrillos indicated satisfactory weather conditions in the "hills." The only other source of essential weather information was an occasional telephone contact over a sub-standard circuit with someone living in a small village in the rugged pass on the Chilean side of the Cumbre. When such a contact was made, the person at the other end of the line usually turned out to be someone without knowledge of weather conditions or other helpful information. It so happened in this case—Captain Robinson was unable to make such a contact.

The apparent flyable weather in the "hills" began to rapidly deteriorate as the flight entered the Pass. Atmospherics in the high mountains is anything but stable—it changes with the rapidity of an electric light bulb responding to the flip of a switch. Shortly after Captain Robinson entered the Pass, he reported to Santiago, a sudden and extremely heavy snow storm had been encountered and which appeared to be rapidly increasing in intensity as the flight neared the Cumbre. Shortly afterwards he advised that both sides of the vertically walled canyon pass had disappeared from view, that both of his outboard engines and the nose of the plane were almost entirely obscured by the swirling mass of driving snow. A moment later a further report said that the storm had forced him to abandon his attempt to cross into Argentina and that he was returning to Santiago. Captain Robinson's final report stated that the return route to the west and safety was also blocked by the storm—that he was "on instruments" and thought his position was on the Argentine side of la Cumbre. There was no further report.

Sometime later during one of my search flights I found what appeared to be oil residue, smudges, and other impact marks of the crash on a vertical granite mountain wall at approximately 21,500 feet elevation just south of the statue of Christus de los Andes near the Cumbre. Captain Robinson was indeed on the Argentine side as he had surmised! Evidence indicated that he had attempted to negotiate the narrow passage through a deep U-shaped saddle in the mountain range but had missed the opening by a couple of hundred feet. After the terrific impact of the heavy aircraft and cargo, the *San Jose* dropped down vertically for more than 3,000 feet where the wreckage came to a temporary halt upon a steep ice-covered granite slope. The severe snow storm continued for almost three weeks. Mountain ranges and wreckage of the lost airliner were buried beneath more than 400 feet of fresh snow.

The pall of thick snow covering the tomb of the *San Jose* and its victims gradually became glacier-like—a huge block of ice. It became thicker and thicker as more layers of snow were piled upon it as the storm continued. The airliner would have remained buried for all eternity except for a most unusual weather phenomenon—a protracted period of extremely warm temperatures during the mid-summer months of December and January. Snow fields and glaciers began to gradually melt from the higher temperatures and to slush their way downhill. Dry river beds became filled with tumbling, cascading, and churning waters which flooded

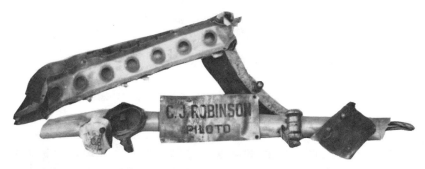

The search for the San Jose *ended.*

The San Jose *had been found.*

large sections of the Argentine countryside where the torrents emerged from the mountain canyons.

The weighty mass of a sliding glacier produces a massive grinding action upon everything caught between it and the earth beneath. The *San Jose* and its occupants suffered that fate. Remnants of the wreck finally became revealed amid the moraine which the glacier had deposited as it slushed its way downward. Gold prospectors, seeking a mother-lode "find" in the upper Andes (a further incentive of a 25,000-peso reward for discovery of the wreckage added to their zeal!) had come upon a piece of an aircraft engine in a crevasse of the high range. Further up at about the 17,500-foot level they found remnants of the victims and airliner scattered amid the boulders and jagged rock residue left by the glacier. The long air search was at last over with their discovery. Three surface expeditions into the rough terrain of the high mountain range were necessary before remains of the victims could be retrieved. The first two (I was with the first group) were caught in a sudden heavy snowstorm which could easily have lasted as long as the fatal one which trapped the *San Jose*. Both attempts failed to reach the wreckage—a hasty retreat in both cases had to be made to keep from being trapped on the unprotected mountainside by the driving and thickening fresh snow. The third attempt succeeded in reaching the scene but only remnants of the victims could be found and recovered. No trace of the valuable platinum cargo was found nor was any of the airmail and express. As far as it is known that part of the *San Jose's* cargo still remains in the high Andes buried beneath the ever-forming un-weighable mass of a new glacier.

Wreckage lay where it had remained hidden for three years under the snows of Aconcagua.

Wreckage was scattered for miles down the slopes of Aconcagua.

Pack mules brought out the remains of the passengers and crew.

Palm-Shimmering,
Fun-Loving, Need-Nothing,
Spooky-Voodoo Panama!

SEA PLANES ACROSS
THE EQUATOR

The flight north from Santiago to Panama followed the same route as our flight of four years before, when we first flew to Chile. But during those four years, air transportation had taken on a whole new color, for more sophisticated planes had higher altitude range. Above the clouds lay smooth sailing, and greater speed. All one needed was an oxygen tube between the teeth, and one arrived at his destination a day earlier. I heard of even more sophisticated planes in the United States that were equipped with pressurized cabins, where no oxygen tubes were needed, for oxygen was automatically supplied throughout the cabin. To me, this sounded dangerous, for I knew only too well that one can burn his lungs with too much oxygen.

We flew high. For many hours we slid smoothly in the sunshine and saw nothing but clouds beneath. But, as the hours passed, those beautiful clouds became look-alikes, monotonous, uninteresting, and boring. I had looked forward to seeing the coastline and to skimming the water along our way. But now that was a thing of the past. In 1935 air transportation had but one God, the God of Speed, who ruled supreme.

God of Speed, hasten my journey, away from the

violence of the High Andes, to the serene safety of tropical Panama!

The second day of the flight in Ecuador, Madelyn sat beside me, reading a funny book in Spanish. And as we approached the Equator she said, "Mommie, I want to slide!"

"You remember that! Madelyn, that was four years ago!"

How could we forget! The ROYAL SALUTE TO HIS EXALTED MAJESTY, MIGHTY GOD OF THE SEA, NEPTUNE.

I remembered her screaming, "Daddy's going up over Zero again to slide down the other side!"

And when he had passed over the Equator and had straightened out to fly right, she kicked and screamed, "I want to slide some more!"

"Madelyn, you are too old to kick and scream!"

"I know."

We tightened our safety belts and looked for a place to hold, but as we crossed the great line Zero, Donald slowly and almost imperceptibly dipped the airliner in salute to the Mighty God of the Sea, Neptune. Madelyn said nothing. I was relieved. All three of us were older—and wiser.

At the end of the fourth day, tired and weary, we arrived in Panama and landed at France Field.

Back again in my beloved tropics! Beautiful palm-shimmering, fun-loving Panama! The sky full of Army and Navy planes, diving, rolling, side-slipping, spinning. The bay full of ships, flying flags of all nations. The streets filled with giddy-laughing tourists.

Beautiful need-nothing Panama! No need for clothing or shelter in Panama's gentleness and warmth. No need for labor, the jungles were full of food for the taking.

And spooky, ghost-story, Voodoo Panama! Some white ones called Voodoo "nonsense." But those who had not encountered its powers could disbelieve, if they chose.

Beautiful palm-shimmering, fun-loving, need-nothing, spooky-Voodoo Panama! And now this was our home.

There was no place to live in Panama, for the Canal Zone was for the exclusive use of U.S. Government employees. Panagra provided no housing at all for its personnel, and it was scrounge as we could to find shelter. However, many companies did provide housing for their officials, and we were fortunate in renting the house owned by the North German Lloyd Steamship Company, while their representative was on a six months vacation.

I forget their names, if indeed I ever knew them, for we met for the first time at the door as they were leaving. She was so happy to be going back to the States for six months. "My clothes are hanging in the closets. Wear them if you like. Toodle DO!" And she was gone.

It was a most pleasant house, with garden. There were many coconut trees that constantly swished in the wind. There were many blooming trees, and even more blooming vines. And there was a twenty-foot-wide porch that surrounded the entire house. Away from the icy winds of the Andes! Always a warm gentle breeze of the tropics! I adored my porch, and bought hammocks, rattan sofas and chairs, rented a piano and put it there (with heater inside, to keep the keys from swelling and sticking in the dampness). And I filled the porch with aquariums for tropical fish. It was a beautiful time for me.

Donald had not taken a vacation since he left the States, years ago. And Mr. Harold Harris, vice-president of Panagra, put it bluntly, "Don, take it or lose it. That is company policy."

"I'd hate to lose it," Donald said to me.

"But where will we go? What will we do? Where on earth is it lovelier than Panama, where we are?"

He said he could buy a cruiser and he and I could go to the Pearl Islands for a couple of weeks.

"A hundred miles off shore! In a cruiser! Ah, honey! That's too dangerous! I'm afraid to do that!" I was to learn that I had good reason to be afraid.

He bought a cruiser, the *Icy V*, from General Lewis Brereton, commanding general of the U.S. Army Air Force in Panama, who was being transferred. It handled exquisitely, as one would expect of a cruiser owned by the commanding general.

Madelyn was in a glee. She scrubbed the deck, she polished the chrome, what there was left of it, for the salt air had made away with such finery. In the afternoon, when we were underway in the Chagres River, she spotted an empty dugout in the mangrove swamps. "Daddy! I found a dugout!"

"Madelyn, honey, that dugout belongs to an Indian. It's tied to a tree." She was positive that I was mistaken. "Daddy, please, go get my dugout. Please."

As the bow of our cruiser, now named *La Manana,* edged cautiously into the mangrove swamp, she caught the dugout with a boat hook and proudly proved me wrong, for indeed it was not tied to a tree. And her father agreed with her that it belonged to no one. No one would have wanted it, for the bow was gone, broken off, rotted through. It was worthless, but not to Madelyn. She made it fast, back aft, and we towed it along. Now we were a two-boat family.

Her new treasure, named *Chaggy* for the Chagres River where she found it, lurched and lunged in the wake, like a tarpon lure, and she begged to ride in it.

"But, honey, it's rotten! It will sink with you."

She appealed to her father, who cut the motors and

let her climb into the dugout and cast off.

She found a floating piece of driftwood for a paddle and in a twinkling of it, was in midstream. "Oh, Donald! You are not going to let that little girl paddle in that bowless rotten dugout! Here comes a motor boat!" I screamed, "It will swamp her!"

"Let's see what she can do," he replied, "I won't let anything happen to her." He slipped off his shirt and stood alertly ready for rescue.

The wave hit *Chaggy* immediately. Instinctively, having no bow, Madelyn turned stern to the wake and rode the dugout as she had her bucking pony Tony. From her bucking *Chaggy* she waved triumphantly to her father, who grinned his approval and put his shirt back on.

OH! MY! Our fearless little daughter!

PEARL ISLANDS

Vacation time had arrived, and our cruiser was ready for shove-off. Gas, oil and food were aboard for the long stay. The fresh water tanks were full, a three-hundred-pound block of ice filled the cooler. Everything was ship-shape and the motors hummed in perfect synchronization. Anchors aweigh! Just Donald and me. A vacation!

On the first night out we swung at anchor off the Pacific coast of Panama; and then, just before dawn, we pulled anchor and headed southwest into the ocean. Barring trouble, we would reach the Pearl Islands before nightfall, which was important, for cruising through coral reefs after dark was dangerous.

Within the hour the sea was everywhere. The horizon surrounded us, and I remembered all those years in Chile when I could never see it, for the Andes blocked the curve. Beautiful Horizon! And the blue-blue Pacific was serene.

"Sweetheart, I'm dogged tired," Donald said to me. "I was up all night checking the anchor. I'm going below and catch some sleep. Take the wheel."

"Ah, Honey! In the middle of the Pacific! What do I do if we get in the trough of a wave! We'll be swamped! Don't leave me here all alone!"

"Head into the waves, watch the compass. Don't get off course. When you sight land wake me up."

"I wish I hadn't come on this vacation! I'm afraid!"

He said he liked me when I was afraid, and he went below.

"If you sleep all afternoon you won't sleep tonight!"

He said he didn't want to sleep tonight.

Dangerous vacation! For hours and hours, out of sight of land, it wasn't easy to hold a course, for the wind had freshened, swells were hitting us off the port beam and we were rolling like mad. But finally at dusk I spotted land and called, "LAND HO!" Donald came up on deck.

"Captain Sir! I don't like the way this ship is rolling and spilling my tomato ketchup. And I don't like the way you left me alone all afternoon to fight this rough sea!"

He took the wheel. "Sweetheart, in just a minute I'll have you back in between those first Pearl Islands where it's smooth, just as you like it."

"It isn't smooth in between those islands. We will roll and pitch all night!"

But it was smooth, just as he said it was. He cruised in quiet waters, checking and rechecking his charts for the location of coral reefs, and he tested water depths before he let go the anchor and cut the motors. "Get the tide chart," he said, "and tell me the time of low tide."

"Ah, Honey! I don't know how to read a tide chart!"

"Find the day of the month, the column for 'low tides' and read the hour. We don't want to be stuck on a reef in the middle of the night."

There was no use arguing with him. I found the chart and read it. "March eighteenth—low tide—5:48 A.M."

"Good." He pulled on the anchor line. The anchor bit deep into the coral. "We're safe until low tide at 5:48 a.m. Now I can relax and begin my vacation."

Donald tossed pillows on the bow. "Stretch out with me and rest." We lay there, watching the sky. He put his arms behind his head and breathed deeply. "So this is a vacation!"

La Manana babbled in the windrippled cove, as it swung on the hook. It was so quiet, so serene. Coco palms leaning into the wind, driftwood laying on the sandy beach, silver-white in turquoise sea.

I laid still and listened as an occasional wave washed soft glissandos then spilled, almost silently, in a gentle tune of its own. A fish jumped, then splashed back into the water. A gull squawked, complaining that night was near. A coconut tree shook loose a nut that thudded to the coral sand, free at last to roll, to float away with the tide. What in all the world is as silly as a coconut tree! How it rises, in overstatement of height, in a wild adventure of growing. Then how it explodes, backfires, and leafs out in puny stubble. Silly Clown! Coconuts! The world's biggest nut! A man could be killed should a coconut fall on his head. 'Twould be a fancy death for an airline pilot.

Pearl Islands! In slow motion the sky was turning pink, red, lavender, purple, deep purple, dark blue of the night.

"Why on earth did you want to come way out here to this nowhere?"

He jested, close in my ear, "To be alone—alone at last!"

"We surely are! Why are you whispering?"

We were snugly asleep in our bunks when the wind freshened. Even in the cove *La Manana* began to pound. We could hear the combers breaking on the reef. WHOOOM! Donald got up and went to the aft deck. True, we were just off the reef that had risen around us while we slept. Where had all the water gone! He took the boat hook and jabbed for the bottom. The boat hook went down not at all but struck the edge of the reef just below the waterline. We were almost on the reef, almost help-lessly impaled.

Donald started the motors, grabbed the anchor line, tied a float to it, cut us loose and it was out to sea for us. We so barely escaped with our cruiser—with our lives.

Donald checked his watch. "This isn't 5:48! This is 2:14! Let me see that tide chart!"

With a flashlight he read—"Sweetheart! You got the wrong ocean! This is the tide chart for the Atlantic! We are on the Pacific! You got the wrong ocean! You made me almost lose my cruiser!"

He was mad with me. I was sorry I got the wrong ocean. In the dark of the night we battled the Pacific. Un-til daybreak we fought the sea.

At morning the wind subsided and we cruised the cove, trying to find the float that was attached to our an-chor. Finally he spotted it a hundred feet up on the reef, high and dry in the sun. He swam out and retrieved it. "We'll anchor and stay here for awhile," he said. "What a night!"

It was a beautiful cove, more beautiful in the sunlight than it had been in the sunset. "Let's go skinny dipping before breakfast," he suggested. "Last one in has to watch for sharks!" I peeled quickly and was in first. "Wait!" he yelled. "Don't dive! Where are your shoes? You'll cut your feet on the coral!" But I was already in. Who needed shoes? Who wanted feet down in this beauti-ful fish-filled water?

"You know where you are going to get sunburned?" he called.

"You aren't watching for sharks," I called back. He said he didn't see any sharks and that he was coming in too. And he did, feet first, and his heavy shoes carried him straight to the bottom. He stayed there a long time, as was his custom, for he loved the waving fan coral bottom. He broke off lavender fans, brought them up, threw them onto the aft deck.

Beautiful beautiful Pearl Waters! Deep deep I could see silver-gray coral in lacy lumps, schools of small fish swimming unperturbed, bristly shells crawling on the bottom—long slithering tail-like things hanging by their teeth to coral edges. He dived again and caught my feet, pulled me under. The pockets in the coral were filled with glass fish, small, transparent, translucent, blue-green, bones-showing, glass fish, looking as though they had just been made by a glass blower. So unbelievably fragile! I had heard of glass fish but I never had seen them; for they live only in coral coves and will live no other place. It was a rare treat to see them. One must dive and dive again to find their secret cove, for they live only in certain spots—certain small areas of their choosing.

They darted away from me, although they would not leave their pocket in the coral reef. I tried to "shoo" them out of their home water but they cloistered in their coral crevice to wait me out, seeming to know that very soon I would have to get back to my own world, my world of air.

Back on board, we lay on the cushioned bow, salty wet, to dry in the sun. Our world of air, bogged down in sunshine, smelling of jungle flowers and rubber vine, sounding of monkey chatter and bird calls, rustling in the trade wind that suddenly had begun to blow. Pearls! Ropes of pearls! This exquisitely raw world of pearls let me in for a day and brought me a sea-blue velvet mood to wear.

The airport on the equator is listing to starboard.

PROBLEM

So wonderful a vacation! Cruising in warm waters, in between the coral reefs. Skinny dipping in salty sea. Sunning on a cushioned bow, a-bobble on the hook. So distantly removed from violence, crash, and death in the High Andes.

But after three days of this dreamy time, both of us were ready to return to Cristobal. This placid world of vacation, so new to us, had worn itself out and we were anxious to get back to our world of aviation. So we pulled anchor and set sail back to the Canal Zone. The Pacific was like a mill pond and we reached port before the dark.

"I have a unique problem to solve," Donald said to me, while we were under way, headed home. "Remember

256

the little refueling station on the equator, the small shed, floating on empty gasoline drums?''

"The airport at Tumaco?''

"That one. The airport at Tumaco is listing. It needs more flotation, and empty gasoline drums are not the answer. I must think of some other way, a better way to keep it afloat.''

The unique problem was not so much the lack of flotation but the problem of passengers. For, when the Sikorsky landed to refuel, the passengers would crowd against the starboard side of the airport to watch the refueling, to be sidewalk superintendents. Their concentrated weight caused the station to list and dip water. Once a passenger slid off in the hot muddy river and threatened to sue.

Donald bought fishing poles and provided live bait, in hopes that the passengers would spread out to fish, thereby restoring the balance to the station. Passengers did exactly this. They spread out to fish and they caught fish, great big huge slippery ones. That only created another problem, worse than the first, for the passengers were proud of their fish they caught on the equator and they would not give them up. They carried them along with them, in the plane, their trophies from the equator, to be stuffed and hung on the wall when they got home.

The fish were a smelly added weight to the Sikorsky that already was carrying maximum gasoline for the long flight to the next landing. The cabin was hot and the fish were deteriorating rapidly and there was no way to dispose of them from the air. Passengers enjoyed this wacky sport but Panagra personnel took a dim view of dead fish, so fishing poles were discarded. The fun was over. But the problem remained.

How was Donald to know that the solution to this unique problem was on the way—from the South Pole?

ADMIRAL RICHARD BYRD AND THE JACOB RUPPERT

We had been back only a few days when Admiral Richard Byrd, returning from his exploration of the South Pole, steamed into port. His flagship, the *Jacob Ruppert,* so storm damaged, so ice scarred, tied up to the scorching dock in Cristobal. The sun beat the black deck, the black hull drank up the heat and held it, for it was designed to do precisely that. On the stove-hot plankin lay thick-furred Huskies, panting in prostration. Their huge tongues hung, dripping, from the side of their mouths. With eyes half closed, the great dogs suffered in the unrelenting heat.

The ship's officers and crew, physically conditioned to withstand eternal cold at the bottom of the earth, stayed below.

Only a few designated guests were invited aboard the *Jacob Ruppert,* for the arrival at Cristobal was not to be an auspicious occasion: rather, it was to be a few days of quiet, a short respite before continuing on to journey's end in New York City. We were fortunate to be among those few invited.

Admiral Byrd greeted us in his open-shirted informal way, and after a few niceties and some reminiscing of past meetings, the Admiral said to Madelyn, "Would you like to see our penguins?"

"Oh, yes, sir! I never have seen a penguin!"

"They are in the cold storage compartment. Your father can hold you up and you can look through the window to see them."

"Won't they freeze in cold storage?"

"No. They would not live if we took them out. The storage compartment is lined with mirrors. They will die if they get lonesome. They see themselves and feel at home."

Donald said to me, under his breath, "Do you see what I see?"

"What do you see?" I whispered back.

"Over there in the well deck."

I looked. In the well deck lay eight huge steel tanks, each of them at least twenty-four feet long.

"Tumaco!" we grinned in unison.

"Admiral, what do you carry in those tanks?" Donald asked.

"They are empty. We carried fresh water in them when we built Little America on the Ice Cap."

"What will you do with them, now that you probably need them no longer?"

The Admiral knew full well what such a question meant, for he had been all along that road of "scrounge."

"You want them, eh?" he concluded.

"Yes, Sir, I need more flotation for the refueling station at Tumaco."

"They are yours," the Admiral said, with a wave of his hand. And without hestitation the Admiral called seamen, "Hoist those empty tanks, put them on the dock. Captain Beatty will take it from there."

Madelyn and I went below with Admiral Byrd to cold storage and he held her up to look through the window and watch the penguins. But Captain Beatty was too busy to come with us, for he had a problem. Eight mammoth steel tanks lay on the dock and had to be moved immediately. But his problem of flotation at the airport, Tumaco, was solved.

Those tanks, designed for use at the bottom of the earth, the South Pole, were no longer needed there; so they would be transported to the earth's equator to keep the airport at Tumaco afloat.

Division Manager Capt. Don C. Beatty with passengers and Panagra S43 amphibian—"Sikorsky Clipper"—in 1934.

LAUGHING TOURISTS CAME IN PLANELOADS

Donald had a twenty-four hour job, for his daylight hours were filled with airline operations and his nights were filled with entertainment for passengers. Suggestions from Panagra's New York office that certain passengers might enjoy seeing Cristobal were, in fact, firm directives to "meet and attend," to stay up all night, rum, gum, and lime in hand. These most important passengers had braved flying in order to catch a glimpse of Tropical Wild Life. Bored with night lights elsewhere, they envisioned Panama as a new escape, for now the trip from New York could be made in three days as compared with two weeks via steamer. Three days was not too conspicuously long a time to be away from office and hearth.

They came in planeloads. What was NEW! It was up to Captain Beatty to find it. (And it was more discreet that La Senora Beatty go along, initially.)

The Strangers Club served no purpose, at least not theirs, and so we resorted to "Los Dumpos!" of which Panama had many. They were small cloistered places, neither advertised nor ventilated, where the smell of rum mixed with the perfume of powder and grease paint. The performances began after sundown and lasted until sun up.

The dancing girls gracefully did things they shouldn't. There were yellow-heads from Czechoslovakia, sleek brown ones from Hungary, red ones from Spain and of course, Panama's own black. These were beautiful women, collected for expensive tastes, and the traffic in them rotated throughout South America, beginning and ending in Panama.

However, tableaux of platinum blond show girls from the United States upstaged them all, for the delicate-skinned ones, so pink, so powdered, so perfumed, so naked, stood motionless on velvet pedestals. Music played, drums beat, footlights spotted their various fine points. Enthusiastic applause could hold over a tableau for additional minutes or longer.

Night after night we trudged from Dumpo to Dumpo with those very important passengers who, with dough-faced expressions of *blasé*, nevertheless were hot-faced with blood that ran high. There were nights when Jenny Dore herself was on stage. Jenny Dore! That little French spendthrift of energy, Jenny from Barcelona! Who could ask for anything more?

As for me, I never learned anything new, except one thing. I learned that gentlemen, if they had to tolerate wrappings, preferred light-blue satin.

Dumpos! No one had told me, how could I know? One day I drove a shortcut down Bottle Alley. Door upon door, half closed with nailed-up blankets, opened directly on to the street. Signs beside each door displayed large photographs of naked women, inviting "Black and White." Beside each door were lines of men, some young, some old, some in-between, who stood silently, patiently, hang-dog expressioned, waiting their turn. That night I said to Donald, "Why didn't you tell me to stay out of Bottle Alley! I was frightened nearly to death! Suppose my car had broken down!" He was startled that I had stumbled into the red light district of Colon.

Dumpo Panama!

I had seen too much of this Tropical Wild Life. "I'm not going to Dumpos any more," I told Donald. "I'm staying in Mi Casa, like a respectable Senora." And I stayed home, for months and months, as was the custom for ladies in a family way.

Staying at home was not so tranquil as I had thought it would be, for the introduction of air express brought many changes in airline operations. Valuable shipments were coming through the northern division of Panagra, plainly marked, "In the custody of Capitan Beatty." First, a small baby boy was sent to Lima, in the custody of Capitan Beatty.

"What did you do with him overnight?"

Donald said there was nothing to it, he put the kid in bed and slept with him. Diapers and bottles came with the baby. The baby was a cute little friendly chico.

Then a shipment of bees came through Cristobal en route to a government official in Chile, at Valparaiso. They were not "just bees." They were a species developed at experimental laboratories in California. They too were "in the custody of Capitan Beatty." There was no place in the office to keep them, so Donald brought them home for safekeeping, and put them on our front porch. For three days they buzzed in protest, furiously beating their wings against the wire net that confined them. On the third day, they were loaded aboard a Clipper.

There were shipments of replacement parts for Panagra aircraft that had to be transferred from steamer to steamer by crane, being too large to be flown to their destination. A wing for a Douglas DC-3 arrived one morning via Grace Line, and was transferred by crane to the dock. It was urgently needed in Lima, for a Douglas DC-3 had cracked up during the difficult downhill takeoff from the sloping side of the nineteen-thousand foot volcano Misti. Donald stood watch over it, day and night, until it was safely on its way to Lima.

Then there was a shipment of fighting cocks, huge, rare birds, of exquisite plumage, to be delivered to the president of Ecuador. Like the bees, there was no place for them at the office, so the cocks stayed in cages on our front porch, awaiting flight southward. Each morning, as the sun came up, they crowed like mill whistles that blew, and parrots in the jungles screamed answers to the clarion call. Bedlam in the bush! Every parrot in the jungle was crowing. I was pleased when baggage handlers came and loaded the nuisances into a Sikorsky S-38. "Donald, you shouldn't have to bring all these critters home with you," I complained. "You need a freight depot." He said he sure as hell did, and I laughed, because who ever heard of air freight?

There were shipments of spare parts for mining machinery in Chile, too large to be transported by air, that had to be similarly transferred by steamer.

TILLIA

"Little Boys, Dem Easy to Dead."

In this safe, secure Panama, the violence of the High Andes was not to be forgotten, for pilots' wives, now widowed, and pilots' children, now half-orphaned, passed through Cristobal on their sad journey home. They were constant reminders that tragedy would forever and forever stalk those who flew the frozen wilderness of Chile.

First to come was Swede Lindenberg's little two-year-old son, with his broken-hearted mother. We met them at France Field and took them to the Washington Hotel to wait three days for the next flight to Miami. The little boy kept his eyes on the sky, and as a Ford flew over he screamed, "Daddy!" His little finger pointed high to the sky, as high as he could reach. His mother said quietly, "He adored his father and looks for him constantly. He knows some plane will bring Swede back. It was the Ford that set him tingling. The last time he saw his father was in a Ford."

"It is so strange that he knows a Ford when he sees one. He is such a baby."

An army plane zoomed by. "Daddy?" he asked hopefully.

"No, son, daddy will not be home tonight."

Tears! For all three of us, tears. Thank God Donald was out of the High Andes!

There were still more reminders. Captain Peck came through Cristobal in a lead-lined coffin so heavy that it had to be handled by rigging. And there were the very small mahogany copper-trimmed caskets from the crematorium which contained the ashes of pilots killed in crashes. These were kept in the Panagra office, sometimes on Donald's desk, until they could be flown back to the

Donald Jr. and Mary Alice Jr.

States and returned to next of kin.

In this safe, secure Panama there came to us two chubby pink babies, little more than a year apart. They were blond, blue-eyed, curly headed, affectionately named Pancho and Panchita. And, as was the custom in Panama, we employed two nurses, one for each baby. And, as was the custom, every afternoon the nurses bathed and dressed the babies and took them to walk in the park by the waterfront, Louise with my doll-like Panchita in a stroller, and Tillia with my arm-waving, leg-kicking Pancho in a basket. Usually Tillia carried him in his basket atop her head, for she said, "Him love see palm trees." And she admonished me constantly to be careful with him for, "Senora, little boys dem easy to dead."

It frightened me to see her carry Pancho on her head, but she reassured me that was the safest place. All Jamaican women carried baskets on their heads. It was the custom.

Tillia was Jamaican, very small, not young, blue-black. Her hair just off her forehead was white and her features were clearcut and patrician. Her dialect was half Spanish, half British, and she always used the broad "A." She was a silent one and spoke only when it seemed to her necessary. Her love for my little Pancho, though unspoken, was clear to see. But she never fondled him. Little blue-black Tillia—a spooky little one was she, for Voodoo rituals accompanied her many moods.

Black men in dugouts, white men in Clippers: a thousand years separated them.

A ROUTE THROUGH AMAZONIA

Amazonia was ready for the age of aviation but aviation was not ready for Amazonia.

Tremendous interest in air transportation was growing throughout South America, for many parts of the country had inadequate roads, no railroads and few river boats. Air transportation was a sudden boon. Raw products from the jungle were being brought down the rivers by dugouts and shipped to the States by air. It was an unbelievable sight to see naked black men in dugouts

268

transferring cargo to gold-braided uniformed white men in multi-engined Clippers. A thousand years separated them in time, but there was no language barrier, for big silent grins between the men said it all. Naked black men in dugouts, uniformed white men in Clippers, side by side in commerce! Amazonia was ready for the age of aviation.

Senior Captain Don Beatty, Pilot Ott Gardner and Radio Operator W. Brown on arrival at Cristobal, Panama Canal Zone from the Sikorsky factory in Connecticut with the latest of the Clipper ships. Powered with two Wasp engines and constant speed propellers, this larger S-43 amphibian required a crew of three and carried fifteen passengers. She had a cruising speed of 160 miles per hour and a top speed of 182 MPH, and on the flight from the continental US to the Panama Canal Zone, she established a world record—the fastest flight time to date between the two points.

Passenger loads in the northern division of Panama were increasing so rapidly that additional scheduling was inaugurated and two sections of most flights were necessary. But this was not sufficient and airliners of greater capacity had to be procured. Several times within the year, Donald flew to Bridgeport, Connecticut, to fly acceptance tests and to fly S-43 Sikorsky Clippers back to Panama to handle the ever-increasing passenger traffic.

But additional flights and larger planes were not enough. New routes were needed across the continent from the Pacific to the Atlantic, through the Amazon Basin. Donald knew this area well, for he had spent many months surveying this territory, with his Latin American Expedition. This was the route where he had hoped to establish an airline of his own. He had a most accurate map of this whole region, which he himself had drawn, of this land still marked UNKNOWN.

Panagra began negotiations for such a route, but it was difficult, because much of it lay within disputed territory of Peru, Colombia, Ecuador, and Brazil. The first leg of the route, however, was within the territory of Peru, that part beginning on the Pacific at Chiclayo, crossing the Andes and ending at Iquitos, where the confluence of the Rio Napo, Rio Tigro, and Rio Maranon became the Amazon. With sanction of Peru, a survey flight was begun, with Peru's Minister of War, Commandante Canga, accompanying the survey.

Participating in the survey flight were Panagra's President John MacGregor; Vice-President Harold Harris; Captain Donald Beatty, and co-pilot F.J. Rye. The Sikorsky S-38, the *San Blas,* was used for the survey flight.

I do not know how this survey flight failed, for I was not there and Donald did not care to talk about it when he returned to Panama. A copy of the report of the return flight to Panama is included at the end of this chapter (for

270

Her top speed of 182 MPH made it possible to arrive at the overnight stop before the abrupt tropical shift from bright daylight to complete darkness occurred.

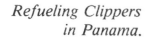

Refueling Clippers in Panama.

*Donald Beatty and Panagra vice-president Harold Harris
discuss route for Iquitos Survey Flight.*

*Panagra's Commodore Clipper at anchor on the Guayas
River off Guayaquil, Ecuador. With ever-increasing traffic, airliners of greater load capacity had to be obtained.*

Panagra at Balboa, Canal Zone, 1934. From left to right: General Manager John D. MacGregor, Vice-president of Operations H.R. Harris, and Division Manager Capt. D.C. Beatty.

anyone who cares to read it). It is the official report to Harold Harris from Captain D. C. Beatty and Mate F. J. Rye.

In general, this is what happened (as it was related to me). The first survey flight into the jungles from Chiclayo to Iquitos was made without incident and the Sikorsky landed on the Maranon River. However, the return flight was ill-fated. There were problems not anticipated, for while the Sikorsky performed with precision in the low altitude of the Amazon Basin, it was out of its element in the thin air of excessive tropical heat, along with the rarefied atmosphere of the Andes. The air was too thin for the Sikorsky to lift off from the hot still waters of the Maranon.

The Sikorsky S-38 (San Blas) *sits helpless in the Maranon River. The air was too thin and the water too hot and smooth for take-off.*

To lighten the load, surplus passenger baggage was put ashore and abandoned. The Sikorsky would not lift. Then, all the passenger baggage was removed from the plane and abandoned. (The men were unhappy about this.)

Still the Sikorsky could not get off the water.

Then all equipment not completely necessary for flight was taken ashore and abandoned. But even with minimum weight, the air was too thin and the water too hot and smooth for takeoff.

With hours of attempt at takeoff, the bow of the seaplane threw walls of water that cut like steel and ripped off the edges of the propellers. This damage had to be repaired before a takeoff could be achieved. With no machine tools and with no hand tools, but with the ingenuity of pioneers, there would be some way by which the survey plane could be flown back to Panama. Donald was sure.

Mr. MacGregor and Mr. Harris left by river boat and at Barranca, a Peruvian Army outpost, a Peruvian military plane brought them out of Chiclayo. Many days later, at the first wind of a cool morning, a wind that rippled the hot still water, Donald finally got the Sikorsky on the step and, as he writes, "squeezed" it off the Maranon River and flew it back to France Field. Amazonia was ready for the age of aviation, but aviation was not of the age to take on Amazonia. (Echo from the Latin American Expedition. Donald found that out in 1931.)

From notes of Capt. Donald Beatty
Iquitos Survey—Amazon River Route

Severe water damage to the propellers during the several attempted takeoffs had injected still another obstacle. Both props appeared to be beyond repair and the nearest replacements were in Connecticut, USA! Ocean travel time from there to Belem at the mouth of the Amazon, then up river 2300 miles on a wood-burning paddle wheel riverboat (it made the trip about once every seven weeks) would take at least three months! The special propellers would mostly likely have to be manufactured, which could extend their delivery to more than six or seven months.

No one was pleased by such a prospect of spending so many months in the middle of the Amazon jungles. I reluctantly chose the only alternative, a "field repair." This required a delicate job of attempting to balance each individual propeller blade, a difficult and precise procedure even with proper tools, facilities, and specialists to do it. With

A wall of spray, flint-hard, cut the prop tips in sharpnel and shot jagged pieces of metal into the hull.

Panagra Vice-president Harold Harris examines damage to Sikorsky.

that decision, props were removed from the engines and damaged portions cut off by hack saw. Deeper pits in the leading edge of each blade were filed in by hammering adjacent metal into the crevices with a ball-pein hammer. Raw edges were filed smoother.

Then balance (?) began by stringing them on a sapling tree, a part of an "A" frame built for the purpose, the sapling being small enough to go through the hub. The delicate balancing thus became what

Repairing the San Blas *in the Maranon River.*

No power tools were available.

was known as a "by God and by damn" type. Additional metal was removed from each blade and its edges again filed smooth until all appeared to be of equal weight. Then they were re-installed on the engines.

In spite of such mutilation of the sensitive propellers, I managed to "squeeze" the survey plan up above 15,500 feet to top of the clouds obscuring the Andes on my successful flight to the Pacific coast and home!

RETURN TRIP OF IQUITOS SURVEY FLIGHT

CRISTOBAL
October 31, 1936

Att: Mr. H. R. Harris
Plane P-23—Captain D.C. Beatty
Mate F. J. Rye

The return flight of the Iquitos/Chiclayo survey did not depart from the former point until 1230 Sunday, October 25th. The filing down and balancing of the propellers was not completed until late during the morning of the 25th, the morning having passed before they were again installed on the engines of P-23. The damage to the propellers caused by water during attempted take-off with a heavy load on the morning of October 24th was a great deal more than was apparent at first examination.

On departing Iquitos at 1230, a magnetic course of 242°30 was followed direct from there to Barranca, a Peruvian Army military outpost located on the north bank of the Maranon River approximately 18 miles due west of the confluence of the Pastaza and Maranon. As the weather was good, with two to three-tenths clouds at approximately 5000 feet, various altitudes from 1000 to 4000 feet were used for the flight, the Rio Maranon being in view to the south the majority of the time.

Arriving Barranca at 1525, a landing was made and the nose of P-23 was run up on soft mud bank out of the main current of the river and at a point where the shore line is indented forming a small cove. The river at Barranca is approximately three-quarter to one mile width, forty-five deep (at the present "low water" condition of the river), and a straight section of the main river suitable for take-offs extends for ten miles.

Refueling was begun almost immediately and was completed some two and a half hours later, a total of 290 gallons being placed aboard. Learning from Captain Moises Vasquez C., commanding the garrison there, that the Maranon at that point had many times gone up or down thirty-odd feet in elevation overnight, P-23 was taken back to deep water and anchored. As a precaution against the anchor dragging, safety lines were taken from the plane to the shore and secured to pilings driven into the ground above high water level. After the plane had been secured, Mate Rye and the undersigned accepted the hospitality of Captain Vasquez for dinner and night's lodging. The accommodations were not good.

After normal take-off at 0825 October 26th, we departed Barranca for Chiclayo, via Borja and Bellavista. A course was laid direct from Barranca to Borjo and, as the weather was more or less the same as the previous day, an altitude of one to four thousand feet was again maintained, the Maranon again being with view towards the south and southwest.

Arriving over the Pongo de Manseriche (a canyon through which the Maranon flows) a long range of mountains running in a northeast-southwest direction was observed. These mountains extend as far as could be seen and were approximately 3500 feet in altitude, their top being comparatively regular and uniformly even. The Maranon river is joined by the Santiago approximately two miles above the upper end of this pongo, the river then spreading to a mile or a mile and a quarter in width before being forced to flow through the narrow canyon through this range of mountains. The canyon or pongo is only 100-200 feet wide and is ten to twelve miles long. At its lower end there are located three or four thatched huts, shown as Borja on the map.

Leaving the Pongo de Manseriche on a magnetic course of 216° direct for Bellavista, we noted that jungle clouds were forming under us, which shortly became large patches of solid undercast. Their altitude was low, however, and the range of mountains running in the northeast-southwest direction was sticking up through these. We continued to see this range immediately on our left for the next fifty miles, when clouds finally obscured same. The weather towards the Andes had begun to look anything but favorable from the time we were over the Pongo de Manseriche at 0920, and when taking the 216 degree magnetic course we had at the same time begun to increase our altitude. When approximately over the Rio Imaza at 1000, Captain Squire, between Talara and Chiclayo piloting Trip 172, advised that the Andes were fairly well closed by clouds. From our altitude of 11,000 feet we could see that with approximately 15,000 feet we could probably pass over the top of the clouds and Andes as the mountains were averaging 12,500 feet maximum altitude at that point. When approximately over Yunguno (10 miles air line down the Rio Maranon from Bellavista) the clouds closed in solid underneath us. Those in front obscured the Andes and were apparently gaining altitude as fast as we were. In order to keep from going "on instruments" over country with mountain peaks of unknown altitude, a magnetic course of 120° was followed for approximately 20 minutes, when same was changed to 270°. As the large amount of metal taken from tips and skirts of the propellers at Iquitos had considerably decreased their efficiency, we had difficulty in obtaining the necessary altitude of 15,500 feet. As the passes were closed by clouds, this altitude was necessary in order to cross over the top. The altitude was finally obtained while on the 270° magnetic course. The consumption of gasoline while dodging in and out of cloud valleys and also while on the 120° magnetic course considerably lightened the plane and permitted us to get on top of the clouds which were at 15,000 feet at that time. At 1145 we were over the west side of the Cordillera and proceeded southwest. The undercast turned to scattered clouds at Mauro, where we had the first opportunity to orientate ourselves. We proceeded to Chiclayo from Mauro where a landing was made at 1239.

The Maranon River from the Pongo de Uthag at the mouth of the river Imaza to Iquitos can be used for landing practically the entire distance at the present time. Extreme care would have to be exercised, however, as the river now, while not at its extreme low, is very near to same.

It appears that the foothills of the Andes extend to a position along a line drawn between Moyobamba and Borja. They terminate rather abruptly from a 2000-3000 ft. altitude along this line. Between there and Iquitos the jungle is perfectly flat, extremely dense and more or less devoid of habitation with the exception of an occasional Indian hut. From Borja the foothills continue on in a north-easterly direction, though instead of being a scattered group of small hills, they continue on as a narrow though definite range.

The section between Iquitos and Barranca appears to be considerably more swampy than that section over which we flew jointly between Moyobaba and Iquitos. Mile after mile of swamp country, with trees, bushes and other jungle growth standing in the water, was observed.

Prior to departing Iquitos, and not knowing whether we would have difficulty with water take-offs on account of our cut-off propellers, I had taken the precaution of securing route maps of the routes Iquitos-Masisea and Masisea/Lima. Should we have experienced trouble with the take-off from the water, it had been decided to proceed to Pucallpa in order to land on the airport there, after which we were to proceed to Pucallpa/Lima. As we knew altitude of 17,000 ft. was necessary for the flight Pucallpa/Lima, we had also decided to check the ceiling of P-23 en route to Pucallpa. As no difficulty was experienced on the take-off, the original route of the return flight via Barranca and Bellavista was followed. We are attaching the strip maps Iquitos/Pucallpa/Lima hereto for your files.

We regret that we are unable to attach hereto photographs made on the return flight from Iquitos. Sgt. Guss of France Field, who does all of our work, developed a bad case of flu after getting the negatives developed and his prints partially completed. The photographs will be completed by tomorrow, however, and they will go forward on the next plane without fail.

PAN AMERICAN-GRACE AIRWAYS, INC.
D. C. Beatty

So it was back to Bridgeport for another Clipper.

But each time Donald flew to the States to bring back a Clipper, he returned to Panama strangely restless and discouraged.

"You should see the airports in the States," he said to me. "Regularly scheduled night flights, landings and takeoffs controlled by radio voice transmission, no more dot-dash telegraphy. They are so far ahead of us that we in South America can never hope to catch up. We are totally out of the mainstream."

"You mean Panagra is far behind?"

"Airplane manufacturing is the exciting thing, new designs, new concepts. You wouldn't believe what Igor Sikorsky has on his drawing board—rotors. He calls them 'helicopters.' Helicopters sure as hell would be useful."

"Helicopter. What a name!"

"I would like to experiment with rotors and with high altitude flight."

"Donald, do you want to go back to the States?"

"I can't go back to the States. This is my job."

It would be nice to go home.

The Santa Maria, *P-33.*

THE STRANGE DEMISE
OF THE *SANTA MARIA*

Spooky Panama! The rainy season had begun. Torrents of water swept the streets as flash floods cleaned away any litter that might have been there. Little naked boys turned cartwheels in the downpours. Parrots screamed and servants said, "Dem calling rain!" Flood tides were with us. Green-yellow skies were above us. We heard Voodoo chants at nightfall. We jested about witchcraft, shivering at the thoughts of it. Spooky, thundering, rain-drenched Panama!

The corduroy road to France Field was several inches under water, and for airline passengers there was a fifty-fifty chance that the bus would drown out in midstream and be unable to continue in either direction. When this happened, passengers had to be carried piggy-back a short distance to the passenger station by the Panagra baggage handlers, Alfred and Horace. But this gamble was an added attraction; for most of the passengers who were traveling by air through South America were doing so largely for the sport of it. They didn't really need to be anywhere by any particular time, and a piggy-back ride simply added to the fun of the trip.

It was on such a rain-drenched afternoon that I drove to France Field to meet Donald, who had taken an unscheduled run to Ecuador with a cargo of replacement parts for a mining company in Quito. He was returning this afternoon. His plane was on time and due at about four. As usual, I arrived about three, wondering why I always came so early to meet him.

It was 4:00 o'clock when I went inside the operations office to ask if the *Santa Maria* was very late. The operations officer was indefinite. "There is very heavy weather south. The radio is not coming in at all. Captain Beatty probably will be late."

It was already late. "How much later? What is your guess?"

His reply was even more vague. I did not like the feeling that was coming over me and my concern deepened.

4:30-5:00. There still was no radio communication and there was no *Santa Maria*.

I had to have some specifics. "How long has Donald been in the air? How much gas is left?"

"He has about an hour's gas. He should be in any minute now."

I walked outside in the slow drizzle, straining my ears

to hear the sound of the motors, that particular sound of the *Santa Maria*, that I had learned to recognize. But all was quiet, save for the splashing of the waves against the breakwater. It was after five. The sun was setting and it was growing dark. I watched the sky and sea merge into one single wetness, until there was no telling where the sky and sea met.

Six o'clock came. Seven o'clock. I bolstered myself by watching the lights come on at France Field. Donald could bring the *Santa Maria* in and land without trouble—if he had gasoline. I was not sure he could have, for the run from Ecuador was a long run and he was late. He was very late. He was too late. He could have no gas left, I could not hope that he had. For I knew that he hadn't. Nobody had to tell me. I could only hope that he was afloat.

The operations officer came to me. "Mrs. Beatty, you should come in out of the rain. Come in the radio shack. We are trying to raise Captain Beatty. He seems to be having trouble with his radio. We should hear from him at any minute."

"Have you had communications with him within the last hour?"

He did not answer.

I went into the shack, the rough frame building, climbed the narrow steep steps to the ten-by-ten radio room, and sat on the top step, close to the operator. The radio key clicked constantly, spelling out the call, "Calling the *Santa Maria*. Calling the *Santa Maria*, Come in *Santa Maria*. Come in. Calling the *Santa Maria*—"

"We should be able to contact Captain Beatty in a few minutes."

He knew that I knew he was lying. He was quiet for a minute, as the key continued to click. Then came the question that I feared to hear, the question that packed the blow, the question I knew would come. "Mrs. Beatty, would you like for me to call Mrs. Dunn to come stay with you tonight?"

The blow itself anesthetized me and kept me on my feet. I answered, "No. Promise me you will not call anyone to come stay with me. I will stay here by the radio where there is communication." My memory flashed me nightmares, a tall brunette screaming at me, "Tell me it isn't Sam!"—the pale face of a platinum blond, too white and still to be alive—a teeny finger of a little boy pointing to the sky and saying, hopefully, "Daddy?" Dear God! Take these nightmares away from me!

"Senora, no one is allowed in the radio shack in such an emergency."

I did not move but sat silently, hoping he would not insist that I leave, according to regulations. He did not press me to go home.

The key continued to click. Intense, alert silence filled the small room as the operator hunched over, closer to the key. The Morse Code slowly clicked the letters, "Calling the *Santa Maria*. Come in, *Santa Maria*, come in—do you read me? Calling the *Santa Maria*. . . . "

A Naval Officer from the Submarine Base came up the stairs, then another, then another. The news was around—Captain Miller of Panagra came and a lieutenant from France Field. No one spoke. The silence thickened as the men leaned close to the key that continued to slowly and distinctly spell out the call. It was a strange and frightening silence, a silence that I never had heard before. I was a part of it.

Suddenly a faint bleep came over the radio. Intense attention filled the room, then excitement spread as the code was faintly clicked out by the *Santa Maria*. The radio key in the shack was silent, to receive the signal that was barely audible. The operator translated the faint signal,

"The *Santa Maria* is afloat. All instruments malfunctioning, out, struck by lightning, the sea is high. The *Santa Maria* is holding up, Captain Beatty does not know his position. He does not know which ocean he is on."

Someone said, "Christ! Is he lost!"

Raucous laughter filled the shack. "Christ! Is he lost!" echoed through the rough framed building. I tried to believe it was funny and somehow it was. Which ocean? I couldn't believe it and since all communications were in Spanish I said, "Please say this to me again, in English. Am I hearing right? Captain Beatty is down on the ocean but doesn't know which ocean?"

"Senora, that is right. Captain Beatty is afloat on the ocean but he does not know 'wheech' ocean." The translation into English made it more hilarious as the officers roared and slapped each other on the back. Who could be as lost as Captain Beatty!

Orders came, "Notify France Field. Notify the Fleet Air Base. Notify the Submarine Base. —Notify New York office, Panagra—"

I remembered once Captain Ennis had jested, "If you ever need the Army, call me!" Captain McWhorter had put in, "I'll do better than that, I'll send the Navy." It was a nice thing to remember, for Donald surely needed the Army and the Navy now. I said again, "Call anyone but don't call someone to come stay with me." The room was filled with levity. Even I had hopes.

I phoned Tillia from the radio shack and asked her to put Madelyn and the babies to bed right away, although it was early for them to go to sleep. "I will be home later. Captain Beatty will not be home tonight, his flight has been cancelled." I didn't want her to know the truth for, if she did, she might go into Voodoo and I couldn't face Voodoo tonight. Not tonight. All I wanted was to lie on the sofa on the porch and wait, alone, for this hideous night to end.

When I reached home the children were sleeping soundly and Tillia was sitting in the back hall on the kitchen stool, with her eyes closed. She was swaying rhythmically, her arms moved as though she held a baby and gently and almost inaudibly she was humming a monotonous chant. Voodoo permeated the air and strangely drew me into its spell. As I stood and watched her, my eyes followed her every move. I floated with her in the rhythm but I knew she was somewhere that I was not. I moved quietly across the porch and lay down on the rattan sofa, buried my ears in the pillows, trying not to hear, not to think. But the monotonous rhythm was quieting to me and I held to it.

Suddenly the chanting stopped and I felt the jolt of silence. Tillia left the stool and went to the kitchen. She returned with a cup of coffee for me and it was hot, very hot. "Senora, him don't coming," she said quietly. I did not ask her how she knew but I too knew him don't coming—forever? forever? Oh, Dear God!

Tillia returned to her kitchen stool and sat there throughout the night, hour after hour and still more hours after hours, as I lay on the sofa, strangely asleep and awake. She sat, gently rocking up and down, humming her weird monotonous rhythmic chant. A numbness was everywhere but I could hear her humming above the numbness. I could feel the rhythm of her swaying. Could she, in some way, be watching the *Santa Maria*? I prayed that she would not take her eyes off the *Santa Maria* and I did not move for fear of destroying something, I knew not what.

Him don't coming.

Dear God! Was this a vigil or a wake? But whatever it was, Tillia's gentle swaying and chanting held the night together and kept it from exploding in my face.

> Him don't coming
> Him don't coming

Hours and hours. Finally, just before daybreak I heard the engines warming up at the Navy Fleet Air Base. I heard the engines warming up at the Army Air Base. The night had ended.

Suddenly planes were in the air, roaring out to sea, roaring in both directions, to the Atlantic and to the Pacific. The search for Captain Beatty had begun. Oh Dear God! The search for Captain Beatty! The past stood before me. The search for Captain Robinson, the search for Captain McMickle, the search for Captain Raley, the search for Captain Sheets, the search for Captain Lindenburg, the search for Captain Harrison, the search for Captain MacMillan. All had been found. There were no survivors. And now, the search for Captain Beatty. I screamed for Tillia. Insane me! To grab for Voodoo. Where were the underpinnings of my own faith?

I heard the roaring sea. I saw floating debris in an oil slick. I saw empty life jackets, a broken tail fin, marked P33. A pack of sharks thrashed the area in a frenzy of feeding. I screamed again for Tillia.

The chant stopped and she came to me. Almost inaudibly, in her complete exhaustion she said, "Senora, him coming." I heard and heard not.

A startling ring from the telephone. I did not pick up the receiver. Another ring. I lay, stunned by the noise. Again it rang. I did not care. I did not move. Tillia picked up the phone and handed it to me. "She here. Her coming." A pleasant voice from the radio shack said the

Santa Maria had been spotted, still afloat, and contact had been made with Captain Beatty. Captain Beatty would fly the *Santa Maria* off the water as soon as Captain Dunn returned with gasoline. Captain Dunn was on his way with five-gallon tins full. Refueling would begin within the hour.

I did not ask where the *Santa Maria* was, nor in what condition it was in. I did not ask which ocean it was on. I said only, "Thank you."

Whose God had heard? My God? Tillia's God? What matter? Some God had heard. I collapsed and wept.

Donald's escapade with the *Santa Maria* became the joke of the day. Was it not funny to have come so close to violent destruction without suffering a scratch or a bruise? The following evening Steve and Marie took us to the Strangers' Club to celebrate. When we entered the club we were greeted with rousing cheers as officers from the Navy Fleet Air Base, Coco Solo, and from the Army Air Base, France Field, rose in boisterous salute to Donald, voting him the champion of all LOST PILOTS.

It was a jolly evening as Lieutenants to Generals, Ensigns to Admirals table hopped, extending congratulations and whacking Donald on the back, offering to give him navigation instructions. But all evening during this table hopping there would slide in a sober moment of wonder. After all, how had he remained afloat? They were serious, for someday they too might have the need to know.

"How did you keep from breaking up on the reef? What sort of anchorage did you use?"

"Holman let out three hundred feet of anchor line, the line never touched the bottom. Could you believe, three hundred feet!"

"What held you?"

"Something sure as hell did."

Nobody knew and nobody cared what I meant when I

said, "Bottoms up to Tillia!"

They laughed, "Bottoms up to Tillia!" and poured more rum-gum and lime.

General Lytle Brown stopped at our table and sat awhile. He asked seriously, for General Brown was always serious, "How did the Sikorsky handle in the water? Did it roll? Pitch? What?"

"It would pitch out of the water then slam back into a wave and shudder, pitch out of the water, slam back. Pitch, slam, shudder, pitch, slam, shudder. Actually there was a rhythm to it. General, it was the damnedest thing I ever experienced."

I said again, "Bottoms up to Tillia!" Everyone laughed and took another drink. Mine was not a drink. Mine was Holy Communion.

That night when we were alone in our pillows I said, "Honest, how did you stay afloat? What did you and Captain Holman do?"

"If I told you, you would not believe me."

"After last night I would believe anything. What did you do?"

"We lashed ourselves in and we went to sleep. We let it pitch. Jesus! Did it pitch!"

"Let's go back to Alabama!" I pleaded. "Let's go home!"

He joked and said that I had too much rum-gum and lime. (I knew that.) "Nothing is going to happen to me. Stop worrying."

"Why should I stop worrying? I don't want a dead husband. Let's leave while the leaving is good. Let's take our chips and go home!"

He said again, "Nothing is going to happen to me. Sweetheart, go to sleep!"

I kept on with my argument although he had dropped off to sleep and didn't hear a word I said.

Neither Steve nor Donald felt that the experience with the *Santa Maria* had been sufficiently analyzed, even though routine reports had been written. They agreed there was something too damned cockeyed about the whole thing and the first night both of them were in Cristobal we would go to the Strangers Club for dinner and rehash the whole incident. Thursday would be the night, for Steve was scheduled in from Ecuador that afternoon.

The sleek Santa Maria, *polished and readied for her last mysteriously tragic flight, waits on a rain drenched cement apron at France Field, Canal Zone.*

Thursday afternoon Donald called me from the operations office at France Field. He hesitated a minute and then asked if I would come out to the Field and stay with Marie.

"What is the matter? Hasn't Steve landed yet? He is late."

"Yes, he is late."

"But why is he so late? I thought he was scheduled in early. Aren't we going to the club for dinner?"

There was a silence. "Why is he so late?" I asked again. "Has his flight been cancelled?"

"Can you come out now?"

"I'm in a wet bathing suit. What is the radio report? Isn't he coming?"

"His radio is out."

"Donald, has anything happened!"

"We're not sure." After a minute he continued, "An hour ago Steve came in for a landing. He was right over the field, then he turned and went back to sea. His last radio message came in so strong that it paralyzed the receiving tubes. He radioed, "Spiralling down—spiralling down—then everything went blank. There has been no further contact. Don't wait. Come on now. Marie is going to pieces."

"Oh, dear God! Not Steve too!"

I went as I was, in a wet bathing suit. Marie saw me coming and ran to meet me. "Steve came in for a landing, so low, right on the ground," she said excitedly. "He was landing, but then he gave it the gun and went back to sea! He was right here! There was no reason for him to go back to sea!" She surmised, half talking to herself, "Maybe he didn't see the ground. He was right here, landing! Do you think he is down?"

I tried to say something that would make sense. "Honey, if he is down he will float all night. Donald will rescue him in the morning. Turnabout is fair play."

We waited until all of us knew there could be no more gas in the *Santa Maria*, that Steve had to be down. I put my arm around her. "Come on, Marie, come on to our house." But she wanted to go to her house. Would I stay with her? "Please don't leave me!"

When we reached her home I could hear the Jamaican servants in the back patio screaming. Lorita, the parrot was weeping and wailing and saying, "Oh poor Senor! oh poor Senor! oh poor—oh poor—poor-poor-poor—" HOW DID THEY KNOW! I went back and pleaded with the servants to be quiet but they held their heads as though they saw horror and continued to scream.

Marie fell across the bed and buried her face in a pillow. Esmeralda came with the parrot cage cover and put it over Lorita, so that she would go to sleep and stop wailing. The parrot was quiet for a time, and then said in a passionate voice, "Good night, sweetheart. Goodnight, sweet—sweet-sweet-sweet—sweetheart!" I could have sworn it was Steve, for it was his voice as only a parrot can mimic. Marie sat up in bed for a brief second then she fell back into her pillow. "Goodnight, sweetheart," she said gently, then burst into hysterics.

We waited for the night to end.

Just before dawn we heard the engines warming up at the Fleet Air Base and at France Field. Suddenly the sky was full of planes roaring out to sea. The search for Captain Dunn had begun.

It was a short search. An oil slick was spotted, surrounded by floating debris, empty lifejackets, a broken tail fin, P33. A pack of sharks thrashed the sea. The *Santa Maria* was down for the second time, in the Pacific, just off the reef. Captain Dunn and all his passengers had completely disappeared. Steve was gone forever.

Dear God! Had I witnessed a Voodoo Transfer of

Tragedy! Had this been meant for Donald!

For days afterward I pleaded to go home to Alabama. "You can't always win! Let's go home on a boat, and never fly again!" My fear of flying had become unmanageable. I felt myself sinking, coming apart, as I had seen other pilots' wives crack with fear.

Then from the New York office of Panagra came a directive saying that the northern division of Panagra would operate out of Lima. I saw it clearly, Donald safety-

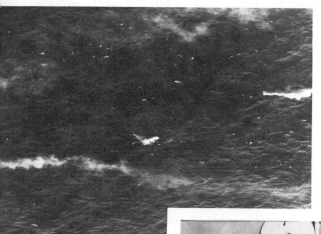

Wreckage of the Santa Maria *was found. Smoke bombs dropped from search planes marked the location of debris floating in an oil slick. Captain Dunn, his crew, and all of his passengers had disappeared—forever.*

U.S. submarines retrieved several mailbags and life preservers from the wreckage of the Santa Maria.

belted to a desk, in a room behind doors marked Management. Suddenly the polarity of my fears reversed. It was no longer the flying I feared, it was the grounding. Was this what I wanted, safety at such a price?

"No!" I said. "We will not go to Lima! If you go there you'll be trapped. You'll never be able to break free from cold, miserable, dead Lima. You'll be tied to a desk for the rest of your life. We'll go back to the States where aviation is alive."

"And give up my job! I can't do that."

"We will not go to Lima!"

Had I ever said "no" to him before? I could not remember a time. "Never in my life have I said 'no' to you," I reminded him. "Well, I'm saying it now. No! *We will not go to Lima!*" He looked at me in disbelief. The night was charged with thinking and neither of us slept.

In the morning he said, "You're not afraid to cast off?"

"No!"

"No job—you are not afraid?"

"No!"

"You won't go to Lima?"

"No!"

"You sure as hell know how to say no!"

He was not unhappy. Had I again said "yes" to him?

On the day of our departure Tillia went aboard the steamer at dock to stay with Madelyn and the babies while Donald and I were toasted farewell by our friends at the Strangers Club. Then we returned to our stateroom, in ample time before the call "ALL ASHORE THAT'S GOING ASHORE!"

Madelyn and the babies were asleep and Tillia sat rocking and humming. I wanted to put my arms around her and kiss her goodby and I believe she knew what I was

Blue-black, white-haired Tillia holds six-week-old Don, Jr. "Senora, little boys, dem easy to dead."

thinking for she stepped back away from me. "Tillia, how on earth will I raise these babies without you!"

"Senora, little boys, dem easy to dead." I promised her I would be very careful with him, and we said goodby.

She picked up a limp pink foot of a sleeping baby boy and held it for a minute in her blue-black hands. Then, so tenderly, she kissed it.

Donald saw Tillia to her cab and gave her an envelope with a check in it, an attempt to show our appreciation. The call came, ALL ASHORE THAT'S GOING ASHORE! The gangplank moved into the hull of the ship and we left South America—forever.

With a ship's steward now watching over our sleeping three, Donald and I went to the bow of the ship and stood in the wind as the prow slit its way beyond the breakwaters and into the moonstruck Atlantic.

"How did we ever get on this silly ship," I said, "this slow, slithering ship glued to a Luna Tic sea? What a dumb way to travel!"

Donald said, "Where are we going? Where does this road lead?"

Leaning back to see the moon that streaked the deck, I said, "Our road jumps over the moon!" And I laughed to think such sport.

"Don't laugh, Sweetheart. It could happen, it could happen tomorrow. Tomorrow the moon."

"When you fly to the moon, take me with you."

And he said he sure as hell would.

THE END.